THE PICTORIAL HISTORY OF WRESTLING

THE GOOD, THE BAD, AND THE UGLY

THE PICTORIAL HISTORY OF WRESTLING
THE GOOD, THE BAD, AND THE UGLY

BY BERT RANDOLPH SUGAR AND GEORGE NAPOLITANO

GALLERY BOOKS
An Imprint of W. H. Smith Publishers Inc.
112 Madison Avenue
New York City 10016

Prepared and produced by Wieser & Wieser, Inc., 80 Madison Avenue, Penthouse B, New York, New York 10016.

Published by Gallery Books, An imprint of W. H. Smith Publishers Inc., 112 Madison Avenue, New York, New York
10016.

Designed by Richard Kubicz

Photographs by George Napolitano, Bill Otten, Koichi Yoshi-
zawa, and Jack O'Shea

Third printing 1985
Printed in the United States of America

Library of Congress Cataloging in Publication Data

Sugar, Bert Randolph.
    The pictorial history of wrestling.

    1. Wrestling—History. 2. Wrestlers—Biography.
I. Napolitano, George. II. Title.
GV1195.S82 1984   796.8′12′0922 [B] 84-20271
ISBN 0-8317-3912-6

This book is dedicated to those wonderful people who make wrestling happen: the promoters, like Jim Crockett, Verne Gagne, Fritz Von Erich, Bob Geigel, Vince McMahon, and Paul Boesch; the thousands of bona fide wrestling stars; and the millions of fans around the world.

CONTENTS

FOREWORD

This book is a celebration of the excitement, the color, the pageantry of America's fastest growing sport, professional wrestling.

Wrestling is the basic conflict between the guys in the white hats and the other guys in the black. It is a conflict that always has been with us. Drawing its vigor and nourishment from its most important element—the fans—wrestling, perhaps more than any other form of entertainment, reflects fundamental codes of morality. Whereas western movies once provided us with the same sense of identification and enthusiasm—provided a medium where we cheered the good guys and jeered the bad guys—now, in contemporary films such as *Butch Cassidy and the Sundance Kid*, we often find ourselves cheering at the bad guys and jeering at the good (good guys, it seems, can also wear black).

This point is hardly lost on the millions of fans who regularly attend wrestling bouts every year—over 22 million in the United States in 1983, according to a Sports Attendance Survey conducted by Triangle Publications. Today, wrestling stands alone as the embodiment of righteous idealism—in America and around the world.

That has always been wrestling's appeal. Wrestling is the most spectacular, and colorful, sport in existence today. It will, we hope, provide excitement for many, many years to come. But here, in *The Pictorial History of Wrestling*, we have tried to capture this thrilling sport between the covers of this monumental book, bringing you the heroes and the villains, the beauties and the beasts, the holds and the acrobatics that can belong to only one sport—your sport, professional wrestling.

GEORGE NAPOLITANO

New York City
August 1984

THE GOOD

ANDRE THE GIANT

IT HAS BEEN SAID THAT WITH great power comes great responsibility. Only one man in the world of wrestling has both: Andre the Giant.

This 7-foot 5-inch, 497-pound giant—a giant among giants in the ring—has only one responsibility in his mind's eye—pleasing his fans. This driving force has earned him millions of dollars and fans, but has also cost him plenty. It has disrupted whatever homelife Andre had, inasmuch as he's on the road almost 11 out of 12 months a year, and it has quite possibly cost him a championship.

Though Andre cannot remember how many matches he has had, he does remember that he has never lost a single one. Then why no championship belt for this "goodwill ambassador of wrestling?" "My schedule demands that I am constantly on the move, and so I don't have time to keep up my regional ranking. I have had some championship bouts, but they either end at the time limit or the champ gets himself disqualified, because he'd rather lose the match than his belt. I can't complain though," Andre continues. "This sport has given me everything I've ever wanted, friends around the world, contacts, everything. I will never leave it."

It is Andre's great love for his public that sets him apart in today's cold world. And for this everyone looks up to the gentle giant of the ring.

Left: Andre has his hands full with a giant supporting cast.
Opposite: Andre applies a painful headlock to the looks and likes of Killer Kahn.

BRAD ARMSTRONG

AT 6 FEET, 225 POUNDS, HAND-some Brad Armstrong is wrestling's version of "Mr. Excitement." Having wrestled professionally for only a few years, Armstrong's skills and dedication have already endeared him to millions.

The son of the famous Bob Armstrong, Brad made his debut on Independence Day, 1980, against Jerry Brown. By 1982 he had been named NWA Rookie of the Year and later became the youngest man ever to hold the National heavyweight championship title.

Brad is impressive, both in the ring and in practice. His accomplishments reflect this. However, the road to the top has not been easy. One of the most disappointing moments in his life came when the relationship between him and his father became strained. Winning the National heavyweight title was not only a personal victory for Brad, but a way of vindicating the Armstrong name. Unfortunately, Brad did not hold the title for long. However, he has now determined to become the youngest man ever to rewin it.

Brad's determination and skills have carried him into and through some of the biggest names in the wrestling world, names like Ric Flair, Ted Di-Biase, and Les Thorton. And with it all he has more than held his own. As he continues on, and continues to excel, there is no doubt that he will be meeting *all* of the stars in wrestling. And that one day he will become one of the brightest stars in wrestling's firmament.

Brad Armstrong makes Michael Jackson (now known as "Mike") sing out loud.

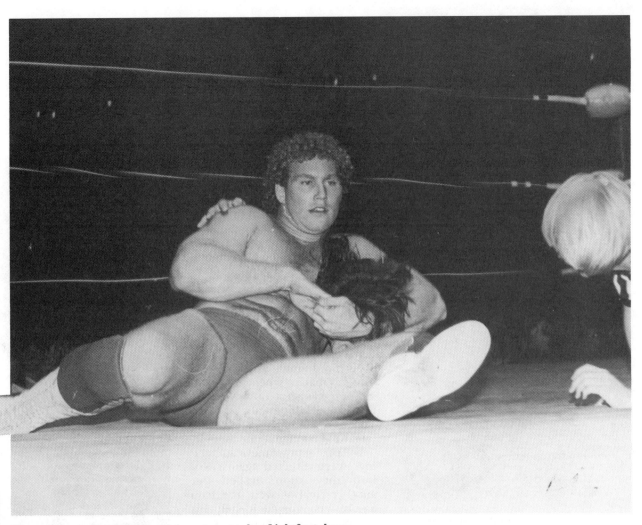

The referee waits while Brad Armstrong takes Lightfoot down.

Armstrong ropes Larry Zbyszko.

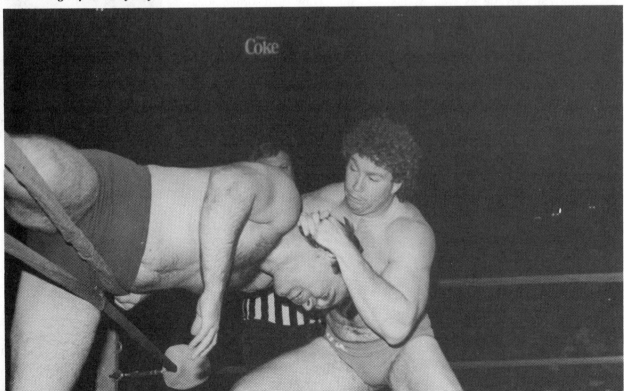

TONY ATLAS

The one and only Tony Atlas shouldering his own world.

TONY ATLAS, MR. USA, IS A body-building champion. And, he can wrestle as well as his great body looks.

After acquiring the title of Mr. USA, Atlas entered the ring and challenged those two villains—and, not incidentally, denouncers of everything good about America—Ivan Koloff and the Iron Sheik. Then he set his sights on the cherished NWA world crown. Facing Ric Flair in Atlanta, he nearly pulled off the victory of the decade, but Flair barely survived, and then, before Tony could get to him again, Ric lost his title to Harley Race.

Atlas refocused on Race, but Race wouldn't even cup an ear to his challenge, telling Mr. USA to wait—or "go fly a kite." Atlas was crushed, his dreams shattered, and his ambition de-stroyed. He knew that he was not only championship material but that he was better than some who were then strutting with their belts. With no outlet for his ambitions, it seemed that he was destined to be the "man who would be king," but never quite make it.

And then Tony heard that Ivan Koloff was making sounds as though he wanted Mr. USA. That was just fine with Tony, who never liked Koloff any-way, taking his insults against the United States as a personal insult. Finally, when a Korean airliner was shot down by the Russians, killing all aboard, Tony made Koloff his personal target for revenge.

If Tony's pro-American feel-ings were directed against Ko-loff, they soon flushed out another rival as well, the Iron Sheik, who vowed to help his friend Koloff "stamp out all American snakes," particularly Mr. USA. They joined forces and burned a path of destruc-tion across the length and breadth of wrestling.

But Tony had other ideas. With "Captain Redneck," he emerged victorious over these two double-dealers in villainy. However, if Tony is going to re-peat his victory, he will now need to team up with yet an-other wrestler of his own high caliber — Rocky "Soulman" Johnson, who has proven himself to be a friend of the USA and of Mr. USA.

Tony Atlas believes in the fu-ture of the United States, and, it is obvious that crowds recipro-cate by believing in Mr. USA, one of the most pleasing per-formers to come along in years. And one who will not only achieve that success he seeks against Koloff again one day, but achieve overall success for years to come.

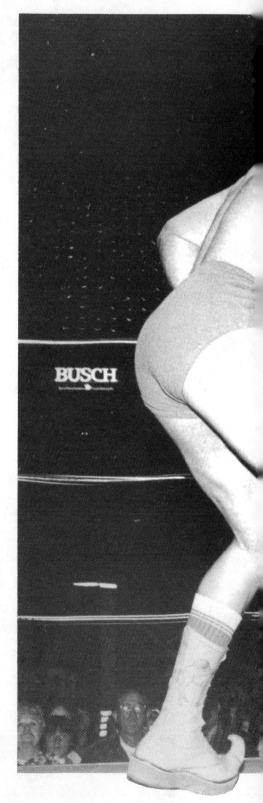

Atlas gives the Iron Sheik the back of his hand—and more.

BOB BACKLUND

Bob Backlund gives Sergeant Slaughter his marching—and flying—orders.

Superstar Billy Graham takes a header.

BOB BACKLUND HAS BEEN wrestling "for as long as I can remember." This becomes evident the moment the good-looking star steps into the ring. He embarrasses his opponents with a wide assortment of moves and maneuvers and usually makes short work of his challengers.

His first exposure to wrestling was early in his school days. He was a natural at the sport and continued with his training throughout his schooling. By the time he reached college, Backlund was so adept at the sport that he was named all-American four times.

The Minnesota native turned professional in 1974, a few years after he won the prestigious NCAA championship. Bob

credits the great Verne Gagne and Billy Robinson with getting him started in his career and giving him the inspiration to pursue his number-one love. The great Danny Hodge was also a big help to Bob in his early days, as were many other fine wrestlers.

During his professional career Bob wrestled in the AWA area, Oklahoma, Texas, Florida, Georgia, Missouri, and the WWF territory, where he established himself as a real star by winning the title from "Superstar" Billy Graham on February 20, 1978.

Watching a Backlund match, one is sure to see Greco-Roman throws, fireman's carries, single- and double-leg takedowns, a vast array of aerial acrobatics, as well as his famed atomic knee drop. This maneuver, in particular, has spelled the end for many of Bob's opponents.

For five years Bob Backlund, "the All-American Boy," reigned supreme and was the toast of the East Coast. He became one of the greatest champions the sport has ever known. During his reign he met and defeated practically every big star in the country. Unfortunately, in December 1983 he lost the coveted title to the Iron Sheik in Madison Square Garden.

Throughout his career he has had victories over Jimmy "Superfly" Snuka; Ken Patera; Big John Studd; the Magnificent Muraco; Sergeant Slaughter; "Superstar" Billy Graham; Adrian Adonis; Greg Valentine; Angelo Mosca, Sr.; the Iron Sheik; Buddy Rose; Jesse Ventura; Ivan Koloff; "Killer" Kahn; Stan Hansen; and many, many others.

Backlund, without a doubt, is one of the top wrestlers in the sport today: he was "born to wrestle."

Backlund has the Magnificent Muraco in an abdominal s-t-r-e-t-c-h.

NICK BOCKWINKEL

Bockwinkel applies a sleeper hold on Black Jack Mulligan.

IF A MOTHER KNEW THAT HER son was going to grow up to be a wrestler, she might want him to turn out like Nick Bockwinkel, perennial AWA champion and gentleman in a sport not known for gentlemanly conduct. Mild-mannered and soft-spoken out of the ring, this quiet stalwart is among the least publicized of wrestling's greats. One of the reasons Nick is often on the short end of the hype stick is because he shuns the antics of his spotlight-crazed colleagues. Some of his best fans, who wish Nick received more in the way of public acclaim, often ask why. The answer is simple. Nick lets his wrestling do the talking. In that regard, Nick speaks softly and carries a big stick, for he is an unequaled master craftsman when it comes to negotiating his way around the ring.

You could say that Nick's ring savvy is his own language, understood in countries around the world, and his international body of fans understands the tongue. For Nick is a prominent world traveler, likely to show up defending his title on several continents in the same week. He is a favorite in Europe, Asia, South America, and, of course, the United States.

Nick has won the AWA title three times. When he first won it in 1975, he set an example for championship behavior by setting off on a title defense spree that lasted until July 18, 1980, the date of his climactic and famous first match with the unparalleled Verne Gagne. In the next nine months these colossuses of the sport met three times, and each time Gagne successfully defended. The series of bouts between the two is one of the most famous in wrestling history. Their last match, on May 10, 1981, was the toughest bout of both men's careers.

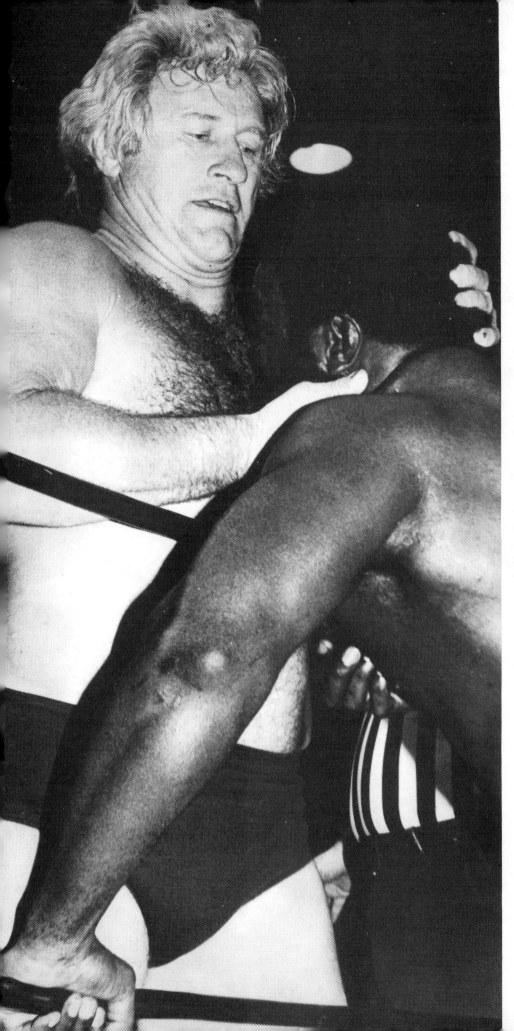

Verne Gagne had announced his retirement and desperately wanted to go out a winner, while Bockwinkel was determined to regain the belt. After a real struggle, Gagne was able to retire with the belt.

The championship committee of the AWA, after many heated debates, finally decided to award Bockwinkel the title after Gagne's retirement. The well-mannered Nick has upheld the honor and dignity of the title and has defended his crown against any and all comers. Every top man in the AWA has been granted a title match with the awesome Bockwinkel, who has methodically defeated them all. Wrestling greats like Greg Gagne, Jim Brunzell, Tito Santana, Dino Bravo, Baron Von Raschke, "Mad Dog" Vachon, Rick Martel, and Hulk Hogan have all tasted defeat at the hands of Bockwinkel.

The only blemish on his record occurred in St. Paul, Minnesota, on August 27, 1982, when he was defeated by European champion Otto Wanz. No one had expected the bloated Otto to take the crown. Wanz' reign was short, however, for a few months later Bockwinkel regained his title. "I chased him around the country till I finally cornered him in Chicago," says Bockwinkel. From August until February 23, 1984, the champion defeated everyone thrown in his path. But, finally, in Tokyo, Bockwinkel met his match in "Jumbo" Tsuruta, the man who finally pinned Bockwinkel's shoulders to the mat. Since then Bockwinkel has tried to regain the AWA crown, and with his experience and ability there is little doubt he will. The rest will be history, as Bockwinkel expects to reign for some time as champion supreme.

A little face lifting is in order for the Junkyard Dog.

19

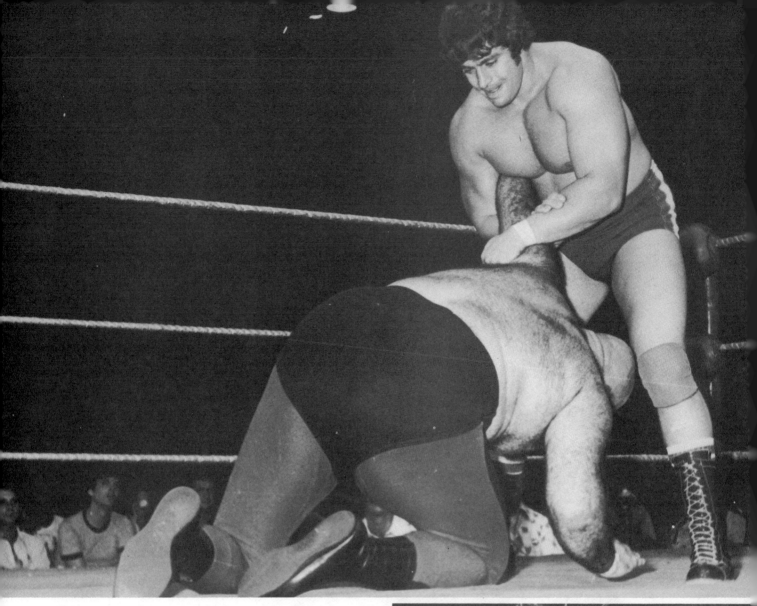

Above: Dino Bravo bends the arm of George "the Animal" Steele.
Right: Bravo slugs Pierre of the Lumberjacks.
Opposite: Dino Bravo applies his patented airplane spin.

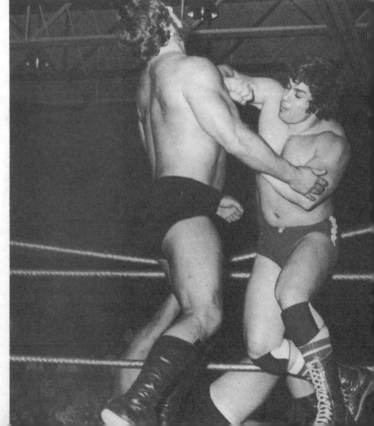

DINO BRAVO

HE COMES FROM MONTREAL and he has been in the business for 12 years. Dino Bravo, the International heavyweight champion, has one thing on his mind—to win the world championship.

Bravo holds two non-title victories over current world champion Nick Bockwinkel, yet shots at the world title have been few and far between. He entered the WWF in 1978, hoping for a crack at "Superstar" Billy Graham's gold belt. But a few days before Dino's match with Graham, Bob Backlund won the title. Dino remained in the WWF with hopes of a scientific match against Backlund for the title, but that match never came about. And so Dino teamed up with Dominic DeNucci to capture the WWF tag team championship. Dino was no stranger to the tag team scene; in fact, one of his first titles was the American tag team title, with partner Victor Rivera in California.

But Dino was unhappy wrestling in tag teams. He was true to his commitment to DeNucci, though, and continued to defend their title. It was no great disappointment to Dino, however, when they lost their title to the Lumberjacks. Dino was now able to return to singles.

He racked up a string of impressive victories and was on his way again toward a title match. Yet, once again, being the good guy that he is, he found that he was being passed up for the rule breakers.

Disgusted, Bravo left the WWF and traveled to the AWA. Anxious for a match against AWA champion Nick Bockwinkel, Bravo signed up for as many matches against top contenders as possible. After an impressive Death Match victory over "Crusher" Blackwell, he was granted a non-title bout

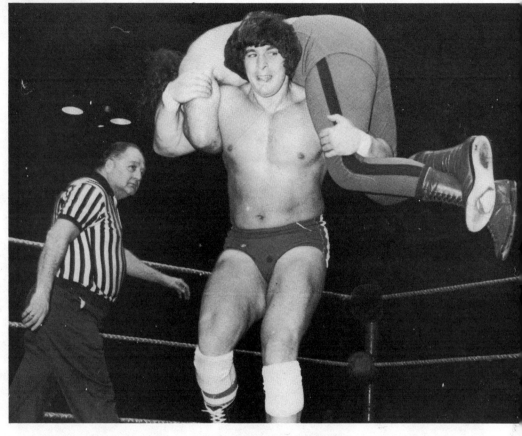

with champion Bockwinkel.

Bloodied and behind for most of the match, Dino rallied in the end and upset Bockwinkel with his favorite airplane spin maneuver. After that, a series of title matches was set, but Bockwinkel's manager, Bobby Heenan, was forever in the way and kept the handsome young Italian-Canadian from getting his hands on the belt.

Dino, disgusted with this situation, headed back to Montreal. There he earned a title bout against International heavyweight champion Michel DuBois. Dino took the crown and went on to defend it against such obnoxious rule breakers as Big John Studd, Lord Alfred Hayes, "Frenchy" Martin, and "Mad Dog" LeFebre.

In 1982 Bravo lost the belt after a particularly vicious blood-

bath with Abdullah the Butcher. The Canadian Wrestling Alliance thought Bravo's behavior during that match was unfit for a champion, but as Dino explains, "I was just trying to save my life!"

Among his many challengers has been his close friend Rick Martel. The two literally grew up together and have been the best of friends for years; they even teamed up together on occasion.

In 1983 Bravo crossed paths with Nick Bockwinkel once again—this time in Montreal. Dino pinned the champion but, as always, it was a non-title bout.

He is a fine young wrestler, he plays by the rules, and he likes to win. One of these days Bravo will win his rightful championship.

BRUISER BRODY

THERE IS NO TOUGHER OR more powerful wrestler on the wrestling scene today than Bruiser Brody, a dynamic and versatile performer—if not, as some of his critics hold, a brutal and animalistic one as well. The power of this 6-foot 8-inch, 320-pound monolith is awesome, even legendary.

Brody has successfully wrestled throughout the country, in the course of his travels holding such titles as the Western States heavyweight, the US tag team, the Florida heavyweight, the Texas Brass Knuckles, the Texas heavyweight, the Texas tag team (with Kerry Von Erich), and the much-prized International heavyweight.

The Bruiser is endowed with superhuman physical qualities. His size alone is a threat to his opponents. But when it is combined with his enormous knowledge of the sport, he becomes almost unbeatable—as Dory Funk, Jr., found out in a wild melee in Tokyo. And Brody's ego is equally enormous, making it impossible for him to conceive of ever being defeated. Suffice it to say, this has not necessarily endeared him to fans. Afraid of facing no one, the Bruiser is self-assured, even abrasive, in his attitude, holding that "no one is bigger or badder" than he is and "no one can beat me!"

Brody's accomplishments speak for themselves without even the Bruiser embroidering upon them. He is a dominating force on the wrestling scene. More often than not, this man who can do anything, does anything, resulting in one or both contestants being disqualified.

The Bruiser feels that he is the "very best" in the sport. He may well be right. He has the size to back that up and is not afraid to use it.

Bruiser Brody applies a super-flying knee to the features of "Superfly" Snuka.

The Bruiser in all his glory—and beauty.

JIM BRUNZELL

Above: Brunzell happily bruises Brody.
Opposite: Jim Brunzell cradles Sheik Adnan el Kassey in a headlock.

JIM BRUNZELL HAS BEEN WRES-tling in the AWA for quite a number of years. And, during his time, the good-looking Minnesotan has become the toast of the Midwest. Brunzell has spent most of his career as part of a tag team with close friend Greg Gagne. Together, these two talented wrestlers, known as the High Flyers, amazed their legions of fans with their sensational wrestling skills and overall expertise. The High Flyers captured the AWA world tag team title on three different occasions and defended their title against every top team in the world.

After wrestling in the AWA for five years, Brunzell left the area and settled in the Mid-Atlantic territory. This move was probably the best thing that could have happened to Brunzell. De-

termined to shed his image as only a tag team participant, Brunzell worked hard to prove to the fans that he was equally as good in singles competition. He finally proved the point by winning the Mid-Atlantic heavyweight title.

With the newly won title in his more-than-competent hands, Brunzell found his claim to being the king of the mountain challenged by everyone who wanted to scale the heights occupied by Jim. He successfully defended his title night after night against all. But, as all good things must come to an end, Brunzell's end came at the hands of veteran great Ray Stevens on Thanksgiving evening. Crushed, Brunzell immediately mapped out a plan to regain *his* title. And, on Christmas Eve, he took the title back

as an early Christmas present to himself.

After wrestling in the Mid-Atlantic area for close to a year, Brunzell returned to the AWA and, in a matter of months, succeeded in regaining the AWA tag team title with longtime friend and partner Greg Gagne. "I enjoy wrestling with Greg," said Jim. "We've been together ever since we started in the sport, and we will always be friends."

Jim Brunzell has proven that he is just as good as a single as he is as a member of a tag team; in all probability, he will always be wearing a championship belt around his waist. The high-flying Brunzell has handled his success very well. With his scientific ability, his experience, and his great dedication, he is destined to become one of wrestling's major forces.

CARLOS COLON

Below: Colon has "Crazy" Luke Williams going every which way but the right one. Opposite: Colon throws Ernie Ladd head over heels.

UNIVERSAL CHAMP CARLOS Colon is a wrestler who rose to the title from the streets of the Big Apple. Although born in Puerto Rico, Colon moved to New York with his family at an early age, and it was there that he learned the tricks of his trade. Colon-izing the universe for the past 20 years, he has learned from the best, and his unique style is a compilation of the finest techniques.

Wrestling professionally since 1964, the Puerto Rican sensation was introduced to the mat scene in 1962 at the late Antonino Rocca's amateur club. Two years later, at the age of 16, he turned pro and has been at it ever since.

It was a tough grind for the young man, but with each success his confidence grew. Colon soon captured the Canadian heavyweight title, the Georgia heavyweight title, and the Southwest belt. After a successful ten-year career in the United States, he traveled to Puerto Rico and since has been wrestling frequently throughout the Caribbean.

To become Universal boss, Colon defeated Ric Flair in the Hiram Bithorn Stadium in San Juan, Puerto Rico. The two had faced each other on several previous occasions, with both the NWA and WWC titles at stake, but in neither instance had anyone emerged victorious. This

deadlock was finally resolved when, in a no-time-limit bout, Colon's patented flying moves and fiery competitive spirit enabled him to upend Flair and earn the Universal laurels.

Since winning this honor, Carlos Colon has charted a formidable course through wrestling waters. The fierce Colon has combined his quick aerial attacks with his relentless fervor to gain victories over many of wrestling's top contenders, including Roddy Piper; Dory Funk, Jr.; "Bruiser" Bob Sweetan; Sweet Daddy Siki; Kendo Nagasaki; Abdullah the Butcher; Ernie Ladd; Ivan Koloff; and countless others.

In the last several years of his wrestling career Colon's toughest opposition has come from "Rowdy" Roddy Piper, Abdullah the Butcher, and, of course, the notorious Ric Flair. Colon insists that "Flair is without a doubt the ultimate wrestler." Twice the two fought to an hour draw. Finally, Colon defeated him to win the Universal title.

Colon admits that Roddy Piper was another tough competitor, but of all the men he has faced over the years, Abdullah the Butcher is beyond compare. "He is a fighting machine," says the well-seasoned Colon. "I've had more battles, more bloodbaths, more *scares* from Abdullah than any other wrestler. He is the wildest, most insane wrestler that I have ever encountered. He can wrestle, too," Colon adds, "when he wants to."

And Carlos Colon can wrestle when he wants to, too, and has accomplished quite a bit himself as a wrestler. This fiery Puerto Rican from the streets of New York is living proof that with hard work and perseverance, virtually anyone can make it to the top.

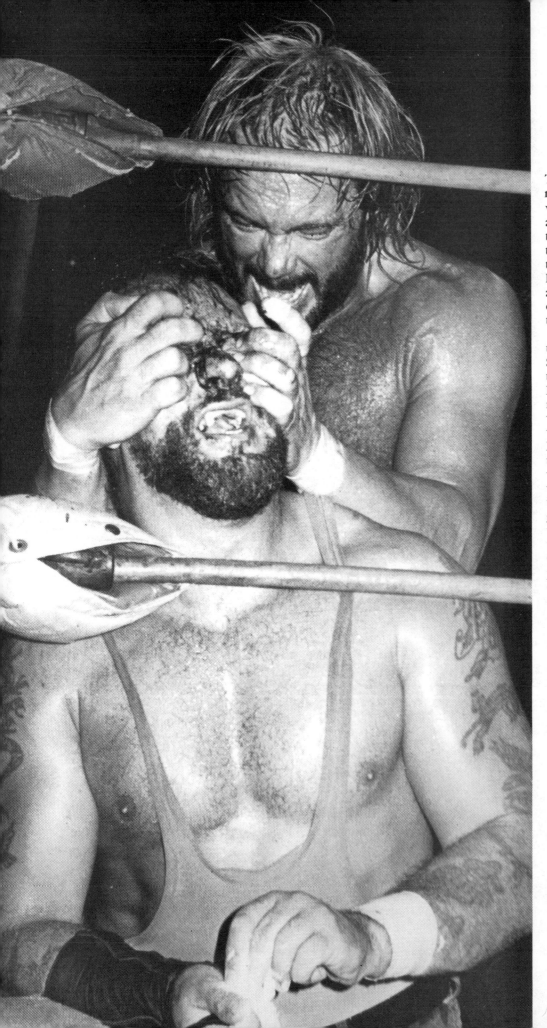

THIS IS THE STORY OF A META-morphosis—of two established wrestlers who, with the help of an old veteran, have changed their image to become perhaps the greatest wrestling unit of the 1980's. Stan Lane and Steve Keirn have put on their top hats and sequined jackets and become a butterfly of a tag team—the Fabulous Ones.

Looking back at the individual careers of Stan Lane and Steve Keirn before they made their miraculous change, Steven Keirn began his professional career in the early 1970's. He wrestled in Florida for several years, teaming with good friend Mike Graham to form a sensational duo. Every title they wrestled for they won. After a while, however, Steve decided to go solo and move on to bigger and better things. He racked up a number of titles, including the Florida championship, Georgia TV title, and the US junior heavyweight title. However, in each area in which he competed he would inevitably fall back into the tag team scene. Clearly, Steve had to make a big decision—tag teams or singles? The answer was obvious, and he soon began looking for a perfect tag team mate. He tried many different partners, and eventually, he found the man he was looking for—Stan Lane.

Stanley Lane, also known as Stan "the Man," began his professional career in 1979, under the watchful eye of former NWA champion Ric Flair. His rookie year was a hard one, but Stan stuck with it. He became a wrestling gypsy, traveling around looking for the best competition. He finally settled in the Sunshine State and won the state's tag team championship with Bryan St. John. What was impressive with that team was the fact that they held the belts

THE FABULOUS ONES

for nearly a year, defending against heavy competition.

Like Keirn, Stan eventually won the US junior championship, Georgia junior title, and TV championships.

In the beginning Stan and Steve were bitter enemies. Manager Jimmy Hart brought Lane into the area with the promise of money and fame, and he made a great contribution to Hart's "First Family" by combining with Koko Ware to win the Southern tag belts from Bill Dundee and Steve Keirn.

Although the fans didn't like his allegiance with Hart, they enjoyed the way the young Lane wrestled, mixing karate with aggressive scientific tactics. But soon Lane himself became fed up with his manager and, on television, fired Hart. This angered Hart, who sent his troops after Lane. Several of the South's favorites came out to help Lane, including Steve Keirn.

The two then joined forces and were going great guns when suddenly they both disappeared; the fans were heartbroken. About this time Jimmy Hart came out with a new tag team known as the New York Dolls. They dressed in tuxedos and top hats and carried canes, and they managed to anger everyone; the fans absolutely hated them.

Then, out of hiding, emerged the Fabulous Ones, complete with top hats, sequined jackets, and real class. They outshone the New York Dolls by a mile, becoming known as the Tom Sellecks of the wrestling world. Female fans fainted in the aisles whenever they entered the ring.

With the original and legendary Fabulous One, Jackie Fargo, as their manager, the Fabulous Ones couldn't lose. They wrestled as good as they looked, and their tactics were unbelievable.

Opposite: Steve Keirn gives "Crazy" Luke Williams a facial. Above: Stan Lane applies pressure to a leg once belonging to Adrian Street.

After conquering Mid-America, the Fabulous Ones set out on a world tour. Their fans were hurt and disappointed, feeling that their team had deserted them. But the Fabulous Ones had to prove to themselves that they were a topnotch combination. Their travels took them to Texas, California, Colorado, and even to the Orient. In each stop along the way they piled up impressive victories. Finally, after being on the road for nearly a year, the Fabulous Ones made a triumphant return to Mid-America. "We want to be recognized as the best tag team in the sport," states Steve Keirn. "We have the magic, the drive, and the pride to take us all the way to the top," adds Stan Lane. And they certainly have that special charisma to get them there.

Gilbert with an armlock on Curt Hennig.

ALTHOUGH EDDIE GILBERT stands only five feet nine inches, he casts a mighty shadow in the ring, longer by far than his size, and one that eclipses that of larger but less gifted wrestlers.

Gilbert's style and grace in the ring are those of a true professional, of any size. They come from years of study, primarily at the knee of his father, Tommy Gilbert. Watching his father wrestle, young Eddie would go over every move he saw his dad make. It was a lesson that he learned well. As he grew up, he translated his study into an ambition: to become a wrestler, and a topnotch one at that.

It was only a short hop, skip, and hammerlock from a successful amateur career to a professional one. Soon Eddie was wrestling in the Central States, in Tennessee, and in Oklahoma, with a brief tour of the Caribbean—and he is now a part of the WWF tour. And if, as they say, travel is broadening, then Eddie Gilbert broadened his horizons with several titles won in several places—like the WWC junior heavyweight title, won in August 1982, and the American tag team title, won in tandem with his father in a bout against the wild Moondogs.

Eddie and his father made a winning combination. Together they won the US tag team championship, the Southern tag team title, and the North American title twice. Eddie also teamed up with Ricky Romero to win the Central States tag team title, with Rick Morton to win the Tri-State tag team title, and, most recently, with Tommy Rich to form a combination known as the New Fabulous Ones.

In 1982 Eddie was ready to try wrestling on his own in sin-

EDDIE GILBERT

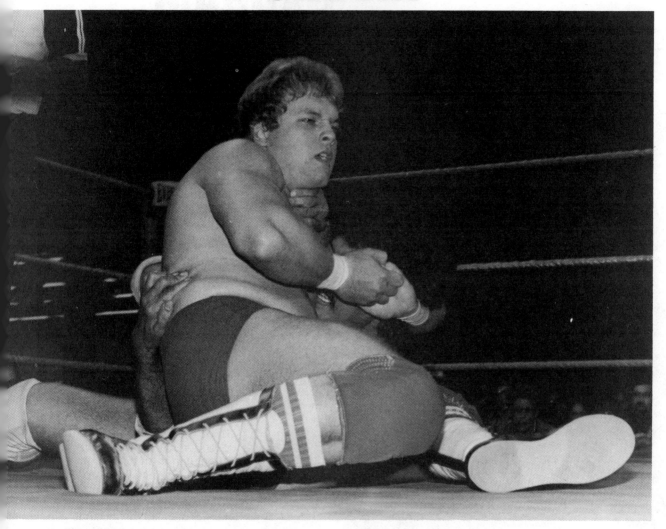

Eddie Gilbert puts the squeeze on Wild Samoan Afa.

gles competition. He was more than holding his own in a highly competitive field when in May 1983 he was involved in a near-fatal auto accident, suffering a broken vertebra and other back and spinal injuries. Eddie made a remarkable recovery against unbelievably difficult odds and came back to make his wrestling dreams come true.

For a short while before his accident Eddie formed a tag team partnership with Curt Hennig. They were dubbed the Super Kids by the press. The kids had a lot in common: both had fathers who were famous

wrestlers and had grown up in similar circumstances, and both loved to travel and see as much of the world as possible. Despite the fact that they made an excellent combination, however, they, too, went their separate ways in search of fame and fortune.

Fate is a funny thing. For Eddie's first match in Madison Square Garden was against the same Curt Hennig. It was a classic, as both of the Super Kids used all of their scientific knowledge of the sport and their mastery of the ring, if not each other, in their efforts to win.

After some fast and furious action, the crowd-pleasing match was declared a draw, much to the delight of fans of both.

For Eddie the chance to wrestle in Madison Square Garden, that emerald palace of dreams, was his dream come true. But, knowing Eddie Gilbert, it won't be the last of his dreams he makes come true. Don't sell him short!

MIKE GRAHAM

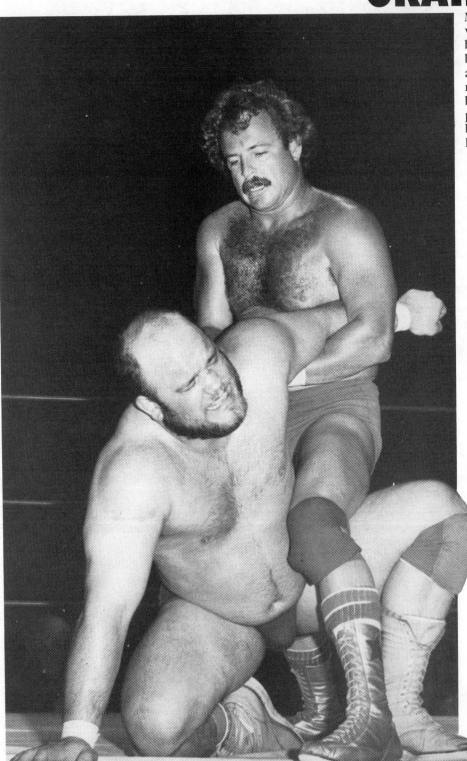

MIKE GRAHAM HAS BEEN IN-volved in many controversial battles in his ten-year career, but none have been as vicious and violent as those in his most recent past. In 1982 J. J. Dillon's black ninja, Kendo Nagasaki, put him to the test in a terrible battle. Nagasaki used his illegal karate moves to severely bruise Mike's esophagus and rupture veins in his throat. Mike was out of commission for several weeks after this unfortunate in-cident. When he healed, he was ready for revenge.

Graham had been well trained in the scientific aspects of the sport, and his father, the legendary Eddie Graham, had taught him how to defend him-self against street brawlers as well. The next time he met Na-gasaki he was ready. "I will make J. J. Dillon and the black ninja pay for the suffering I have endured," Mike threat-ened. And he kept good his threat, literally wiping up the floor with both Dillon and Na-gasaki. Finally, presumably after enough punishment from Gra-ham, Nagasaki disappeared from Florida, leaving Graham to look for other scores to settle.

Graham soon became in-volved in another controversy. His old friend and former part-ner Kevin Sullivan was the ad-versary this time. Graham and

The disarming Mike Graham has an armlock on Buzz Saywer.

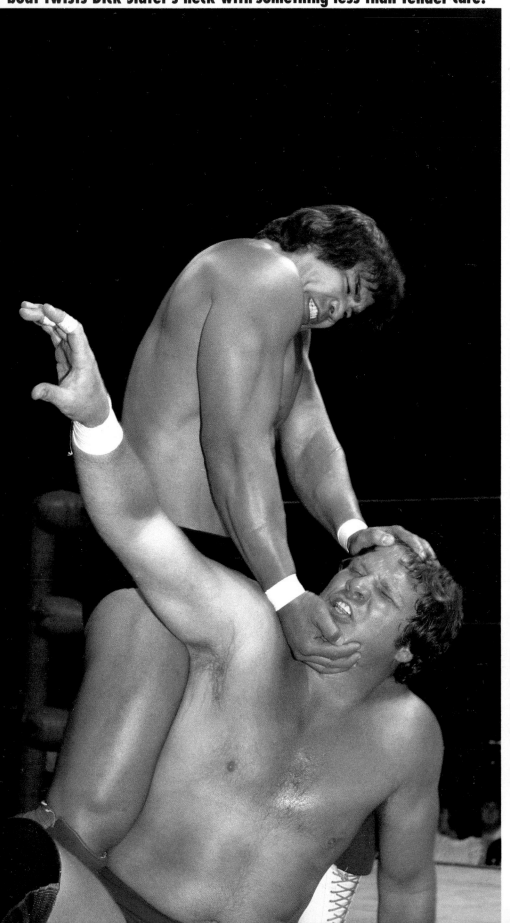
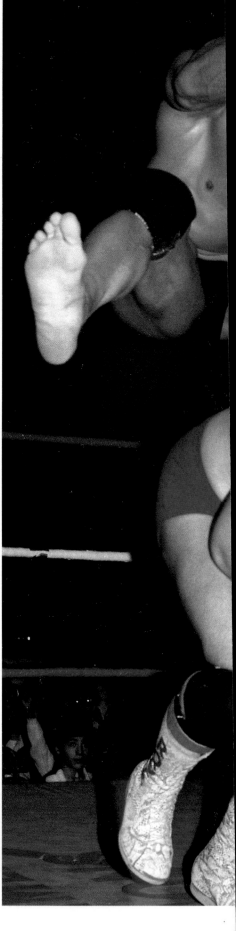

Left: Jimmy "Superfly" Snuka jumps over "Playboy" Buddy Rose, who seems to be held up by legs of little use to him. Below: Ric Flair catches Steamboat in an abdominal stretch.

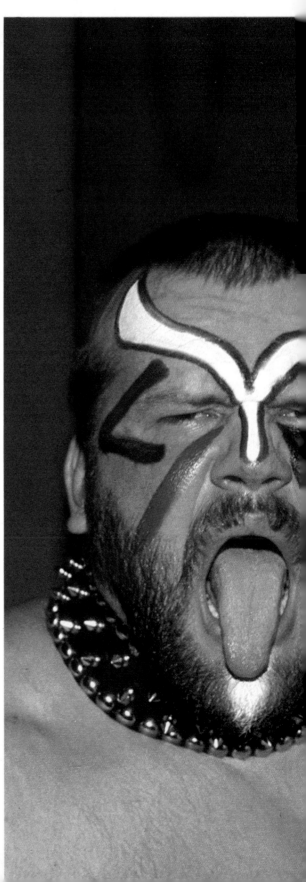

Above: Kerry Von Erich has Ric Flair trapped in his own abdominal stretch. Right: The Road Warriors—Animal and Hawk—show what they think of most of their opponents.

Above: "Boogie Woogie Man" Jimmy Valiant is ready for action—any and all action. Right: "Freebird" Michael Hayes has Don Kernodle in a painful headlock.

Above: Mil Mascaras and Dos Caras, two of the most popular—and most muscular—wrestlers in the sport. Following page: It's none other than Andre the Giant, applying the pressure to Abdullah the Butcher, who has his head trapped in—and on—the ropes.

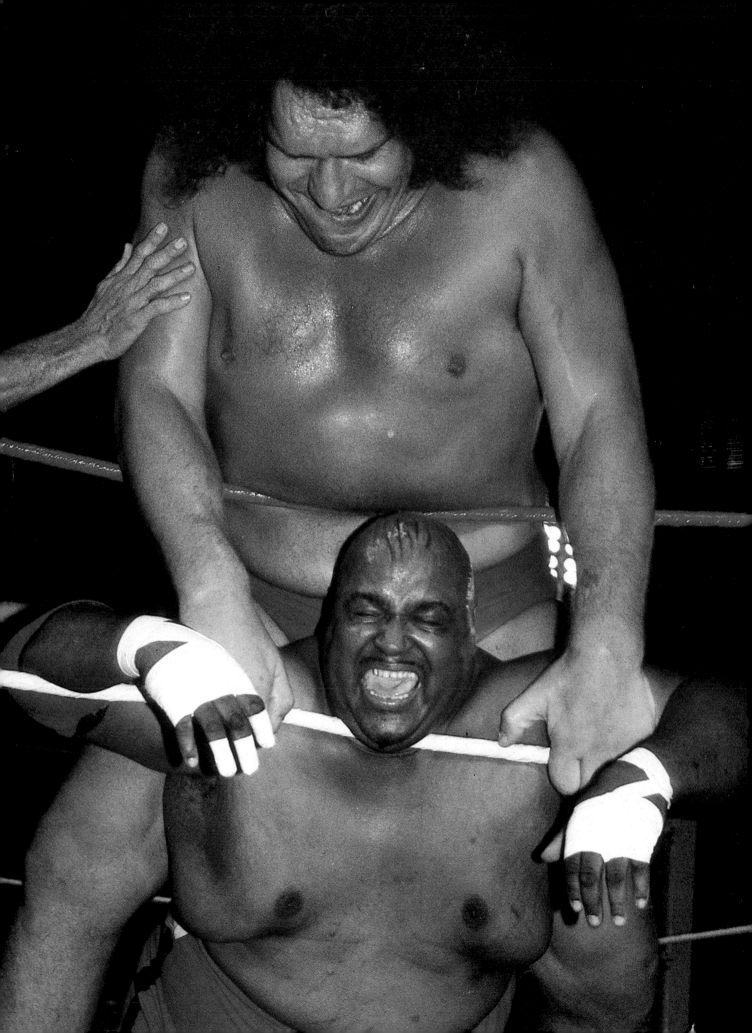

Graham steadies and readies Sawyer for a final fling.

Sullivan had been close friends in 1973, swimming, scuba diving, and working out together as much as possible. They held the Florida tag team title and defended their belts strictly by the rules, using only scientific tactics. However, eventually Kevin left Florida and, through his travels, he changed. When he returned, Sullivan looked like the same old likable fellow, but his actions soon proved differently. He defeated Barry Windham to win the Florida heavyweight title, and his actions after the bout are what set off the raging vendetta with his onetime friend Graham. After Sullivan won the belt from Windham, Graham ran up to the side of the ring to voice his displeasure over the tactics Sullivan had used. Sullivan promptly clobbered him over the head with his victory belt, knocking Graham out cold.

Since then, Mike Graham and Kevin Sullivan have been anything but friends. They have faced each other in the ring on several occasions, and each meeting has resulted in all-out war.

Although he is quite involved with his war against Sullivan, Graham has still found time to challenge Ric Flair for the NWA heavyweight title. Graham holds many non-title and disqualification victories over the champion, and many fans feel that by rights Mike Graham should be champion, but such is not the case.

"This is my dream!" says Graham. "If I could only face Flair in a no-disqualification match, the title would be mine. I'm not ever going to give up," he threatens.

Mike is a determined man. He's a battler who doesn't settle for second best. He plays by the rules, and he will win!

33

HULK HOGAN

HULK-A-MANIA IS HERE TO stay! Hulk Hogan, the awesome, 6-foot 8-inch, 325-pound native beach boy of Venice Beach, California, has body-slammed his way into the hearts of millions. From his portrayal of Thunderlips in the movie *Rocky III,* to the defeat of the Iron Sheik to capture the coveted WWF belt and become the tenth champion in the WWF's 20-year history, Hulk Hogan has been a wrestler to be reckoned with.

Hogan began his career in 1976, when Fred Blassie, the once-great wrestler turned manager, saw Hogan and convinced him that he would make a great wrestler. Hogan signed with the infamous Blassie and went into training. After six months under the manager's iron hand, Hogan was ready for the mat. Blassie began showing him on small cards, and in 1979 he brought Hogan to the WWF area. The Hulk was on his way. Being associated with Blassie made Hulk an instant villain, but he still awed the fans. He was big, he was strong, he was good looking, and he was rough.

But it takes charisma even to be hated, and the fans saw something special in Hulk Hogan. Hulk won his matches easily, and with each victory the big blond became more of a hated favorite.

After his stint in the WWF, Hogan traveled to the AWA. Since he had been a noted rule breaker in the past, he expected the fans to boo him immediately. But from his very first mat appearance in the AWA, the fans cheered the Hulk. Now managed by "Luscious" Johnny Valiant, Hulk battled many rule breakers, such as Ken Patera, "Cowboy" Bob Duncum, "Crusher" Blackwell, and Sheik Adnan el Kassey. With each match he became more popular.

Above: The incredible Hulk Hogan throws Black Jack Mulligan for a loss. Opposite: Strong Kobiashi is Hulk Hogan's private landing strip as the man who invented Hulk-a-Mania takes to the air.

Even after his newfound stardom in the AWA, however, Hogan continued to wrestle as he always had. Unfortunately, he was unable to capture the AWA title from Nick Bockwinkel.

Desiring the WWF belt, Hogan returned to the WWF and decided to take on Blassie's newest protégé, the Iron Sheik, who had just captured the WWF title from Bob Backlund. Hogan wanted to win the belt for the USA, so he immediately began training with Backlund,

who had been injured by the Sheik and couldn't attempt to regain the belt. He and Backlund worked out for many grueling hours in preparation for the bout, and on January 24, 1984, Hogan defeated the Madman from Iran in fewer than eight minutes at Madison Square Garden in New York.

The muscular Hulk knows the fans are with him now and enjoys the cheers. He is big on training, and he knows that it is his physical condition that

keeps him on top. And he likes it at the top! He loves the applause, the money, and the adulation, and you can bet he is going to try to be there for a while.

The Idol of all he surveys.

AUSTIN IDOL

AUSTIN IDOL FANCIES HIM-self to be the nearest thing to a Greek god. With an enormous ego—large enough to be divided into three parts, like Gaul—he boasts of his irresistibility and of the hundreds of women swooning over him. It's not enough he calls himself a ''universal heartthrob,'' he also calls himself a king as well.

With brains, talent, and intestinal fortitude, the Idol has left a trail of broken bones to rival those broken hearts. In the process he has captured the Southeastern heavyweight, the Georgia heavyweight, the National heavyweight, and the Texas heavyweight titles. Everywhere he has gone, seemingly, a belt was there to be had, as he proved as he traveled around the world, adding the Austral-Asian championship belt, the International belt, and the CWA world tag team title to his ever-growing collection.

The Idol gloats over his outstanding successes, often strutting across the wrestling landscape basking in his numerous glories. Modesty has never been his strong point, and wherever a microphone can be found, Idol will be close-by proclaiming his greatness. But there is one thing about which he has yet to boast: the most coveted belt of all, the NWA world title, which has eluded him three times.

Nevertheless, the unflappable Idol will never give up. He believes he is too great *not* to be the world champion someday. And the fans who carry those signs that immodestly proclaim IDOLMANIA FOREVER also believe it. For Austin Idol is one of the more determined men on the wrestling scene. If he can merely get his hands on one of the champions in a title bout, he will break his heart, too, as he has done those of so many women.

Austin Idol captures Animal of the Road Warriors.

ANTONIO INOKI

ANTONIO INOKI HAS BEEN the number-one man in Japan for the past ten years. He began his career in 1961 at the age of 17, and now, 23 years later, the Japanese star is still a force to be reckoned with in the Orient.

As a young boy, Inoki was determined to make it as a wrestler. Although many young Japanese boys wanted to become wrestlers at that time, few actually made it. But Inoki practiced, practiced, and practiced. He studied the Oriental arts of self-defense, including judo and karate, as well as the ancient Japanese modes of self-defense. After one year of intense training, Inoki finally had his first professional match. He then stayed in Japan for three years as a ring boy. Next, Inoki came to the United States to receive schooling in the American art of combat.

Inoki arrived in the United States in 1964 and quickly learned the skills necessary to mix it up with the Americans. He wrestled all over the country on his first tour, grappling his way through Kansas City, Portland, Seattle, across Texas, Tennessee, and California. In Los Angeles, Inoki won his first major title—the America's heavyweight championship.

When he returned to Japan, the young Inoki was considered a star, and soon the Japanese people were hailing him as their number-one hero. His fame and reputation grew as he continued to decimate all the top contenders. During the 1970's Inoki wrestled a tough series of

Above: Hulk Hogan gets a sample of Inoki's best foot forward. Left: Inoki applies his sleeper hold to the Masked Superstar.

Andre the Giant and Inoki in a battle of arms—and wills.

matches with the former NWF champion Johnny Powers. They were gruesome battles, but when the smoke cleared, it was Antonio Inoki who held the NWF title.

With this title tucked under his belt, Inoki was quite secure in his position as the top wrestler in the Orient. But, with this new title, he also found it harder and harder to find the time to travel to the United States to compete, and so, few American and Canadian fans had the opportunity to see this warrior in action.

But many top heavyweights wanted a crack at Inoki's title, so they came to Japan to try their skill against the Saki King. Inoki's most persistent challenger over the years has been Tiger Jeet Singh. Although these two battled many times, Tiger Jeet Singh was never able to upset the talented Inoki.

A few other memorable bouts include a match against Olympic star William Ruska, several matches with kick karate champion Monster Man Eddy, and his fiasco against Muhammad Ali. This last was an over-hyped bomb with questionable rules that left Inoki looking bad next to "the Greatest."

But Inoki quickly recovered his reputation after his bout with Ali, and continued his reign over the Orient, defeating the likes of Stan Hansen, Hulk Hogan, Wahoo McDaniel, Abdullah the Butcher, Andre the Giant, and even Bob Backlund.

Two years ago Inoki returned his NWF crown, hoping to concentrate all his efforts on winning the International Wrestling Grand Prix title. In May 1984 he won the title from Hulk Hogan. Now, fans from all over the world will be able to enjoy this great Japanese wrestler as he travels around, demonstrating his great ability and style.

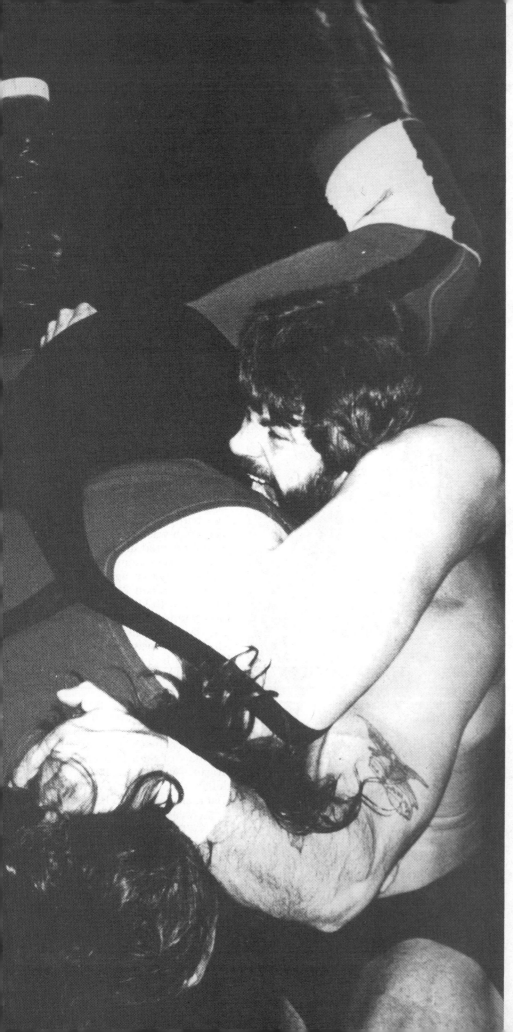

BILLY JACK

THIS MUSCULAR GIANT FROM the streets of Portland, Oregon, has overcome some of life's early bum raps to become one of America's most popular wrestling champions. Modeling his path to glory after the beloved Dusty Rhodes, Billy made his way from humble beginnings and early adversity to the top rung of his profession. He learned the burdens of responsibility while caring for his blind father, and ever since has taken the time to extend his massive reach to handicapped children and anyone else less fortunate than himself.

A superbly gifted athlete, Billy prides himself on a rugged regimen of conditioning. He developed his awesome physique during years of weight training and power lifting. Weighing 255 pounds and standing 6 feet 3 inches, he can wield 480 pounds off the bench press, execute a 640-pound lift, and haul 705 pounds on the dead lift. For Billy, racquetball is an hors d'oeuvre to keep himself at the peak of his prowess. He once won a YMCA racquetball championship by trampling well-honed youngsters half his weight with his finesse and agility. For sheer power, Billy is a titan. He once body-slammed a hapless 450-pound opponent as if the lug were a pound of beef jerky; his versatility always comes as a surprise to bewildered foes.

This combination of dynamic assets has contributed to Billy's impressive string of titles. Starting in his body-building days when he won the Mr. Pacific Coast title, he racked up the Northwest heavyweight championship by obliterating the Dynamite Kid, and after making several ill-fated attempts, he was able to wrest the Florida state heavyweight title from Kendo Nagasaki.

Billy Jack sends One Man Gang up and over.

Billy's forays into Nagasaki country have become legendary. They met first in a cage with taped fists, then in a pit chained together to prevent escape, and even in fearsome lumberjack battles. In each of those events Nagasaki was able, through crude stealth and nuclear-age dynamics, to retain his ill-gotten crown. Nagasaki's day of reckoning loomed, however, as Billy finally dropped the Big One, giving the evil genius his just dessert—defeat. As a sign of gratitude to his supportive fans, Billy dedicated his Florida title to the people "without whose help I couldn't have won it. Nagasaki will never get it back from me now."

Even more amazing was Billy's baptism in the blistering pit of tag team wrestling. Early in his meteoric career Billy joined forces with the former WWF champion Stan "the Man" Stasiak. In the days when Billy had been a nobody trudging the Portland gutters, he had idolized the great Pole. Now Billy, with Stan as his mentor in controlled violence, made the most of a shot at the Pacific Coast tag team titles held by Rip Oliver and the masked Assassin. Thus, less than a week into his tag team career, Billy and Stan beat the demonic duo in two straight falls and carried home the belts.

In the ensuing months Stan and Billy tasted defeat and exchanged the prize belts with the loathsome duo several times, but a righteous precedent had been set. The continuing vendetta between Billy and his nemesis Rip Oliver is one outgrowth of this blood feud. Rip had humiliated Billy by disrupting a radio interview and slapping Billy into his blind father. Billy finally took his revenge when he tore Oliver limb from limb in a brutal cage match.

Billy credits his rapid ascension in the sport to the thoroughbred training he received at the hands of two great trainers, Don Owens and Stu Hart. Under Owens in Oregon and Hart in Canada, Billy developed his techniques and learned the ropes. He proved his mettle in Canada by outlasting a full-ring free-for-all in which 150 fame-hungry gargantuans from all walks of life slugged it out until one walked free. The survivor was Billy Jack. The walking-tall saga, and Billy's one-man assault on the American dream, had begun.

ROCKY "SOULMAN" JOHNSON

ORIGINALLY HAILING FROM Washington, D.C., the 6-foot 2½-inch Soulman of wrestling moved with his family to Canada at the age of 13. Then, it was on to Detroit, Michigan, where he took up karate and boxing. But it was while he was in Canada that the Soulman made up his mind to become a professional wrestler. While training for his amateur boxing debut, several wrestlers in the gym noticed Rocky's superb physique and persuaded him to try his hand at wrestling. By the end of the first day's session, Rocky had fallen in love with the sport, and his boxing days were over.

Rocky Bollie, one of the wrestlers who first spotted Johnson, helped train Johnson at the beginning of his career. It was Bollie, in fact, who gave Johnson the inspiration to become "Rocky" and carry on his great name after Bollie himself suffered an injury to his back that left him paralyzed. When Johnson embarked on his professional career, he took the name Rocky as a tribute to his friend and mentor. (The nickname "Soulman" came quite naturally after Johnson demonstrated his dancing skills on a TV show in Los Angeles appropriately called *Soul Brothers.*)

Rocky made his debut in Toronto, Canada, in 1968 against Firpo Zbyzko in a winning performance under the banner of former NWA world heavyweight champion "Whipper" Billy Watson, who had signed Rocky to a five-year contract. After that first performance against Zbyzko, it was all the way to the top for the Soulman. During the next 14 years Rocky fought thousands of matches, logging hundreds of thousands of miles by car, train, and airplane. He has toured nearly every state in America and has appeared in several foreign countries, including Germany, Korea, Japan, Samoa, New Zealand, Australia, and, of course, the country in which he got his start, Canada.

But it hasn't been all peaches and cream for the Soulman, who has suffered more than his share of injuries during his career. Once, while wrestling the Giant Baba for his PWF championship in Japan, Rocky was on the receiving end of a low kick from the 7-foot, 300-pound giant and was out of wrestling for about two months. Another time, wrestling in Germany, a doctor incorrectly diagnosed a broken rib as merely a bruised rib, and when Rocky wrestled the next night, he was thrown against a table, rupturing the wall of his stomach and breaking even more ribs. "Superstar" Billy Graham knocked out two of Rocky's teeth in 1970, and Buddy Rose knocked out two more several years later when Rocky tangled with him up in the Pacific Northwest. "I've had my nose broken three times and my collarbone broken once," says the Soulman, dismissing his injuries almost as if they were part of the hazard associated with his profession.

"I'm not complaining, mind you," he says, pointing out that he has also endured the normal complement of cuts and injuries to the knees and shoulders. "But a wrestler takes chances and knows on any given night he can get injured." Brave words indeed from a man who knows what wrestling is all about.

Along with the injuries, however, have come the successes. And Rocky has had more than his share of those, too. He has won the America's championship, the US tag team championship (that with Paramount Samoan Chief Peter Maivia), the Florida state tag team championship (twice, with Pedro Morales), the world tag team championship (once with Ben Justice, then with Pat Patterson), the Pacific Northwest tag team championship (with King Parsons), the US championship, as well as the WWF tag team title (with Tony Atlas). Rocky points to Pedro Morales as his favorite tag team partner. "Pedro and I have this certain magic that sometimes happens between two wrestlers. Once we started to train as a team we both knew what we had going for us." That magic has worked many times.

Opposite: The Soulman sends Fuji flying into the cameras. Above: Johnson applies his back breaker to Charley Fulton.

JUNKYARD DOG

UNIVERSALLY LOVED BY ALL, Junkyard Dog is one of the most popular wrestlers in the sport today. And it is a popularity that seems to be growing with each and every bout.

The Dog has fought the biggest and best stars in the profession today. Afraid of no one—or, as they say, "there is no dog in this Dog"—he has approached every bout with a winning attitude and a winning method. Against the Great Kabuki, one of the most feared men in the ring, the Dog went at him tooth and fang, his dislike of Kabuki unleashed in his special, crowd-pleasing style. Once was seemingly enough for Kabuki, for never again has he accepted the challenge of the Junkyard Dog—a wise move on his part. But if Junkyard has his way, it may be yet another Dog-bites-Man story.

Although the Dog has wrestled primarily in the South, winning the North American heavyweight championship and the Mid South tag team title, he now wants to expand his lot. And soon fans all over the country will have a chance to see this exciting personality as he enters the ring and proceeds to get down to business, employing his own brand of dog-eat-dog attack.

No matter what happens, Junkyard seems destined to win. And destined to have the support of his fans behind him every time he enters the ring. It's an affection that's well placed and reciprocated. The Junkyard Dog wants always to please his fans.

No one's meaner than the Junkyard Dog.

Junkyard Dog makes the Great Kabuki heel.

JERRY "THE KING" LAWLER

·The King gives Dick Slater a royal pain in the left arm.

FOR 13 YEARS JERRY LAWLER may have been the most talked about man in Tennessee. During this time Lawler has held every title in the CWA, including the International, the Mid-America, and the Southern heavyweight championships. The "King," as he is known, has also ruled the tag team scene with a variety of partners.

The famous Jackie Fargo was instrumental in the beginning of Jerry's career. While he was doing quite well for himself in Tennessee, Fargo heard talk of a young wrestler with potential. That young wrestler was Jerry Lawler. Fargo went to see for himself and decided to take Lawler under his wing. He trained him well and set him up with his first professional matches. But soon young Lawler's growing prowess in the ring and his popularity with the fans led to an inevitable showdown. At that time Jackie Fargo was the top wrestler in Memphis. When Jerry Lawler upended Fargo, the crowds went wild and dubbed him the "King" of Memphis, a name that has stuck with him throughout his career.

Most of Lawler's activities have centered in the Mid-America area. Although he has traveled to other parts of the country at various times during his career, he has chosen to stay fairly close to home. Throughout his reign he has put many wrestlers in their dutiful places, most recently including Joe Le-Duc, Austin Idol, Randy "Macho Man" Savage, and Jim Heirhart.

Lawler's most persistent adversary throughout his career has been manager Jimmy Hart. Hart has tried all sorts of evil schemes, hoping to drive the King out of Tennessee, but all for nought, as Lawler continuously comes out on top—and comes back stronger than ever.

If fans throughout the world had an opportunity to see Lawler in action, they would agree that he is truly the King of "rassling."

The King in all his royal splendor.

Wahoo McDaniel gets the upper hand in a strap match against Dick Slater.

SIX FEET TALL WITH JET-black hair, dressed in bright reds, yellows, oranges, blacks, and blues, this onetime NFL football player turned wrestler strikes a colorful picture wherever he goes. The native American wrestling great Wahoo McDaniel is a living legend in the wrestling world.

Long before Wahoo was known to wrestling fans, his name was already well known to millions of football fans. He had become a noted star in the pro scene in the 1960's, playing middle linebacker with such outstanding teams as the Dallas Cowboys, the Denver Broncos, the New York Jets, and the Miami Dolphins. Of course, he didn't just start off in the pros, but got his learning experience playing college ball while attending the University of Oklahoma from 1956 to 1960, under the guidance of Bud Wilkinson. Wilkinson was a tough, do-it-my-way-or-else coach, but his toughness paid off and sent young McDaniel on his way to a professional career.

But his football career soon turned him toward another profession. Finally fed up with being traded around like a baseball card, Wahoo hung up his shoulder pads and headed for the mat. He started wrestling part-time out of Indiana in 1960 and took his training from old-time wrestler Johnny Heidiman. Wahoo made his pro debut against Dan O'Shocker—and won. The added fame and money were quite attractive to Wahoo, and he returned more and more often to the ring. It wasn't long before promoters realized the great draw potential of a famous football player–wrestler. Canny promoters soon had Wahoo appearing on cards in the area where he had played football, knowing that fans would be

WAHOO McDANIEL

Wahoo McDaniel flings Tully Blanchard across the ring.

flooding the stadiums to see their local football hero wrestle.

His popularity continued to grow, and after ten years of wrestling part-time he turned to wrestling as his full-time career.

With the exception of that of the AWA, McDaniel has captured championship belts wherever he has appeared. He won the world tag team championship with Tommy Rich in Georgia. He has claimed the Florida heavyweight championship, a Texas state heavyweight championship, the Texas tag team title with Ivan Putski, the Mid-Atlantic championship, the

Southwest championship, and many others. The title Wahoo enjoyed the most was the Mid-Atlantic belt. "It was nice," he recalls. "We were drawing in real big crowds."

There never has been, and never will be, a dull moment when Wahoo McDaniel enters a wrestling ring. He has been in every type of match known to wrestling—from pole matches to street fights, to cages and tag team matches. The fearsome Indian strap match is Wahoo's specialty, however, and he has never lost at it.

But even McDaniel is cautious

of cage matches. "They really tear up your skin. Usually the cages are ragged and made out of wire and pipe, and you know it is really very dangerous to be in one. You also can cut yourself up very badly."

There have been many Indian stars in wrestling—such as Billy White Wolf, the Strongbow brothers, Frank Hill, and the Lone Eagle—but none have gained the fame, fortune, and respect of Wahoo McDaniel.

RICK MARTEL

BORN AND RAISED IN QUE-bec, Canada, Rick Martel comes from a wrestling family. Both his brothers, Pierre and Maurice, were in wrestling be-fore Rick became involved in the sport. Pierre still wrestles in the Caribbean, but Maurice, un-fortunately, died in a ring mis-hap a few years ago. On more than one occasion Rick has teamed with brother Pierre to keep the brother act alive. But it's as an individual that Rick shines. Although his brothers were known for their rough-house style, Rick has ideas of his own about wrestling. He prefers to wrestle by the rules, but he will get tough if pushed too far. Says Martel, "There are many wrestlers who take shortcuts to getting their victories. But I'm proud of what I've accom-plished and how I've accom-plished it. When my hand is raised in victory, I *know* my victory is deserved."

Rick has always enjoyed sports, including hockey, swim-ming, horseback riding—and es-pecially wrestling. In college Rick joined the wrestling team and did quite well, well enough to turn professional at the age of 18. During his ten years of grap-pling, Rick has toured more places than Bob Hope and Bing Crosby ever dreamed of: Aus-tralia, California, Canada, the Caribbean, Germany, Hawaii, Hong Kong, Japan, New Zea-land, Puerto Rico, Singapore, and in the southern and north-eastern areas of the United States—to name just a few.

In his wide travels around the world Rick has gained many ti-tles, including the Australian Commonwealth championship, the Canadian championship, the Hawaiian championship, the Pacific Northwest cham-pionship, the Australian tag team championship, and the Georgia tag team championship (with Tommy Rich). He has also won the WWF tag team cham-pionship (with Tony Garea, twice).

Rick first received national prominence when he toured the WWF territory in 1981–82. It was then that he teamed with Tony Garea, forming what many consider to be the most popular tag team ever to grace the area. Rick and Tony first won the WWF tag team cham-pionships from the Moondogs. Although they later lost their belt to them, they regained it from their adversaries in a match that will be remembered by all who saw it as one of the ring's classics. The two de-fended the title with fierce de-termination and were riding on cloud nine until they lost the belt to Mr. Fuji and Mr. Saito in one of the most controversial matches ever.

Rick recalls the match—and the controversy: "The WWF never should have allowed the belt to change hands. Mr. Fuji tossed salt into my eyes, and I

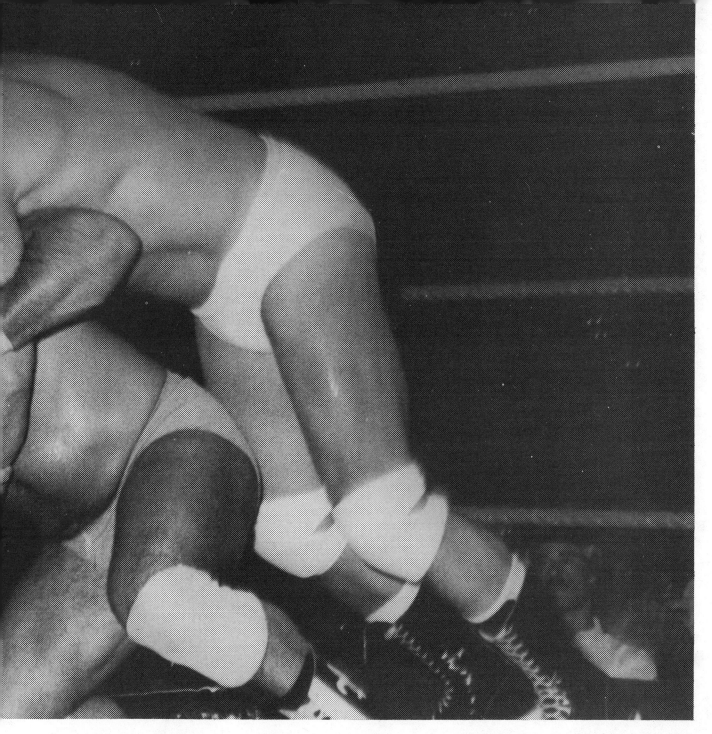

Nick Bockwinkel is taken aback by Rick Martel.

was blinded and easy prey for a pin.''

More recently Rick's career has turned to double duty as he alternates between AWA rings and Canadian rings. Wrestling in Canada, Rick has occasionally teamed up with Dino Bravo, who, not incidentally, also holds the Canadian International title, a championship Rick covets. Professional wrestling watchers believe that a match between the two would be a great scientific contest, one worth waiting for.

Martel has challenged for the NWA world heavyweight championship several times, facing Harley Race as far back as 1977–78 in numerous bouts. ''Race is one tough wrestler,'' remembers Rick. ''Once I held him to a draw in Australia. The next time I came close to winning but injured my knee and was pinned. I wasn't the seasoned veteran that you see today.''

In May 1984, in the St. Paul Civic Center, Rick Martel accomplished his life-long dream by defeating Nick Bockwinkel

for the AWA title. Now that he's on top, Martel should prove to be a very popular and exciting champion.

MIL MASCARAS

MIL MASCARAS, THE MAN OF A thousand masks, is, simply stated, incomparable. He is colorful, dynamic, and sensational. For over 20 years now he has been pleasing fans with his performances. And there is no indication that the Masked Sensation has any plans to stop now.

The hero of all Mexico has traveled the world in the name of wrestling—and of perfection. A great wrestler of world-class caliber, Mascaras has been a huge success in every country he has ever visited.

But of anyplace he has ever been, the world traveler's favorite place is New York. This budding intellectual, who enjoys the sights and sounds of every culture, particularly likes the legendary streets of New York, where he can enjoy the many museums, attractions, and cuisines.

Because he wears a mask in the ring, Mil Mascaras can lead a private life outside the arena, blending into the local scene with many of his fans who do not recognize him. But once inside the ring, the mask becomes a target, not only for the idolatry of his many fans but also for the villainy of his hundreds of foes. And it hasn't been easy, especially since he was targeted for stardom by the Mexican press even before he began his storied career. Mascaras had a lot to live up to, and was fearful that he couldn't meet the high standards set for him. But, true to his greatness, he was able to attain those standards and heights few other wrestlers ever reach as he captured titles, awards, and trophies all over the world.

That's Mil Mascaras, the man in the mask, the man with the famous flying moves—including the flying body block, flying leap, and a wide arsenal of drop kicks and head scissors—who is in a class by himself.

Mil Mascaras takes the Masked Executioner the final mile.

Mascaras puts his foot in Mr. Fuji's mouth.

PEDRO MORALES

PEDRO MORALES IS A LEGEND in the wrestling world, the only living great who has held all three of the titles recognized by the World Wrestling Federation. First, he was the WWF heavyweight champion; then the WWF tag team champion, with Bob Backlund; and then, last but certainly not least, twice he won the Intercontinental championship. Morales is a wrestling star of the first magnitude, one who has lit up the wrestling horizons for years—and should continue to do so—and given every future star a target to shoot for.

But Morales has not always been a star of the first firmament. In fact, during the early part of his career he was forced to live in the long shadow cast by "the Living Legend," Bruno Sammartino. On the night Bruno won the WWF title from Buddy Rogers the young Morales wrestled against Willie Bath. And on the night Bruno lost the title to Ivan Koloff young Pedro played second fiddle to Sammartino, wrestling on the undercard. However, ability will out, and Pedro's did when, one month later, he defeated Koloff for the championship. Now the cameo player had become the leading star in that long-running drama known as wrestling.

However, it wasn't long before the original star, Bruno, faced the new star. That happened in a classic confrontation at Shea Stadium, when Morales faced Sammartino in the pouring rain. But the fans were more than satisfied, even elated. For both had fought with style and determination, as befits men of championship caliber. Both were that night, and will be forever.

Morales retained the WWF title for two years, until he lost it to Stan "the Man" Stasiak, who used his illegal heart punch to overpower the unsuspecting Morales and win his title.

But even that controversial loss failed to deter the fighting heart of Morales, who, wrestling with Bob Backlund, came back to beat the Samoans in a wrestling spectacular at Shea Stadium in front of 40,000 fans. At the time the Samoans were undefeated and had left a trail of destruction that crisscrossed the face of wrestling, much as the long scars they had left on the faces of their helpless opponents. But now the tables were turned as Morales and Backlund never let the Samoans practice their foul tactics, overwhelming them with their skill, determination, and power. It was a night for all to remember!

Within a month Morales and Backlund shocked the wrestling world with the announcement that they were retiring as undefeated champions. But it was a move dictated by Backlund's back-breaking schedule, which made it physically and humanly impossible for him to defend *both* his WWF championship and his tag team championship. And it was in keeping with the team's high standards of fairness—both to the sport and to the fans, who demand that their champions work at being champions and not put their titles in cold storage.

Pedro's great skill and determination paid off again shortly afterward. In a battle with the then Intercontinental champion and Olympic gold-medal winner Ken Patera, Morales subdued his formidable adversary and won the championship. Unfortunately, it was a belt he would soon have to surrender to the Magnificent Muraco. But, truth to tell, the Magnificent One used an illegal foreign object to accomplish his foul purpose. Justice won out, however, and when they met again, Pedro won back *his* belt.

That's Pedro Morales: nobody can keep him down. Just when it looks like somebody or something will, Pedro Morales always comes back. That's what makes a legend! And Pedro Morales is one.

Pedro Morales throws the Magnificent Muraco for a loop.

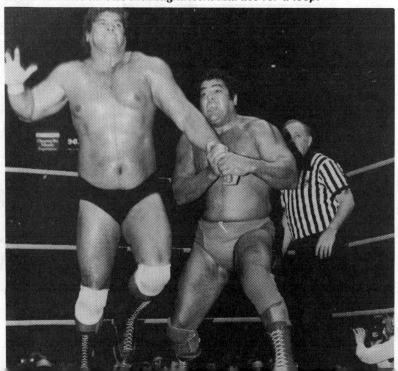

Morales chairs Bruiser Bob Sweetan in San Juan bout.

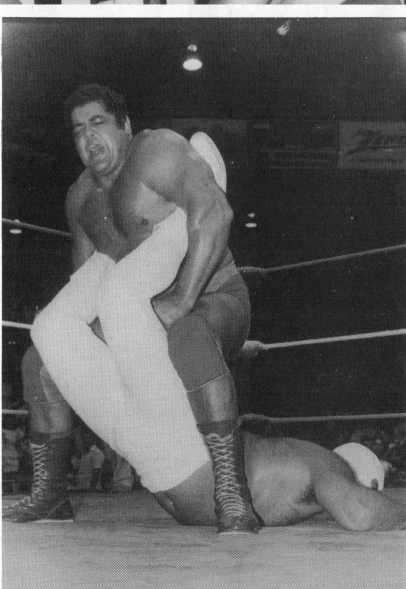

The Medic is in need of emergency help as Morales applies a Boston crab.

ANGELO MOSCA, JR.

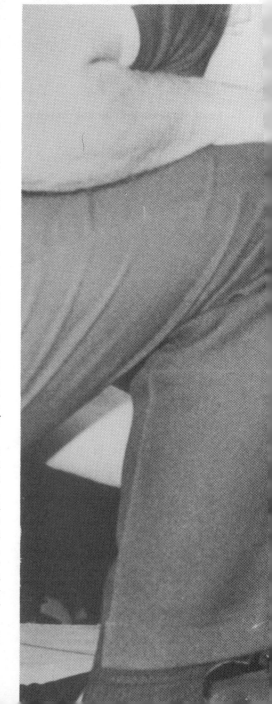

THIS EXTEMELY TALENTED and versatile young wrestler is more than a chip off the old block, he is a block unto himself—as totally different from his father as the words *junior* and *senior*.

Angelo Mosca, Jr., has gone on a one-man crusade to bring dignity back to the sport of wrestling—and to bring that great bear of a man, Ivan Koloff, to his knees.

The story of how he has done both is part of wrestling history. And bears retelling. While waiting to fight Dick Slater for his title belt, Mosca—and the wrestling world—watched in horror as one night Slater showed up on TV and gave away his Mid-Atlantic championship belt to, of all people, Ivan Koloff. How could the arrogant, rule-breaking Slater be so unprofessional as to simply give away his title? everyone, including Mosca, asked.

It was a black day for wrestling, one Mosca intended to expunge. Unlike Koloff, he would earn the belt in the ring, where titles are meant to be won and lost. So, with grit and determination, he set his sights on Koloff. Finally, after the officials of the NWA were besieged with outraged letters and calls, they arranged a match between Mosca and Koloff for the title—to be covered live by TV, of course.

Mosca was confident he would avenge the smear on wrestling's good name. Even more confident that his dad, Angelo Mosca, Sr., would be in his corner. But Ivan Koloff was just as confident. The Russian Bear, no second-class talent, was used to defending titles—whether they were given to him or not. And, he had more experience than his young opponent.

As the two men met in the center of the ring and thousands of fans in the Shelby, North Carolina, arena shouted their support of Mosca, Mosca shouted over to Koloff, "I'm going to take your belt away from you." Koloff merely laughed in the youngster's face. But the smile soon faded from the Russian Bear's face as Mosca slammed

Angelo Mosca, Jr., has Harley Race in his favorite embrace.

Mosca has a handful of Race's face in Norfolk bout.

his fist into the Bear's midsection, all the way up to his wrist. That first blow set the predominant tone for the bout.

Koloff tried every trick in the book, and some that were not to be found anywhere, but the totally prepared Mosca countered each successfully. With fire in his belly and conviction in his heart, he drop-kicked, body-slammed, and tackled his way to victory.

As Junior held aloft his newly won Mid-Atlantic belt, Angelo Mosca, Sr., looked upon the scene with the fierce and noble pride of a father. But the pride was shared by everyone in the arena. For Angelo Mosca, Jr., had brought dignity back to wrestling.

Championships are made to be won and lost in a ring. And Angelo Mosca, Jr., carried his championship, as he does himself, with pride and dignity— pride and dignity that was well earned in retrieving a belt that wasn't.

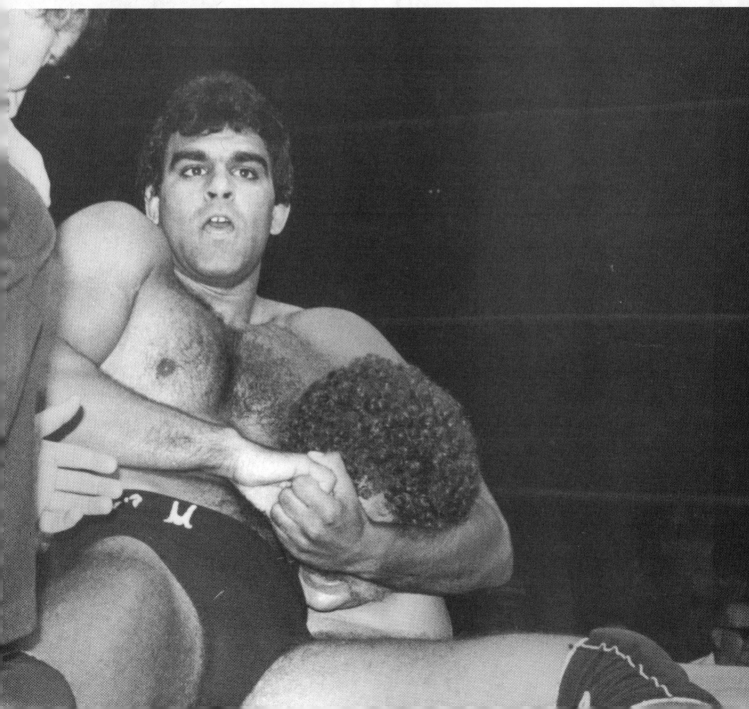

ANGELO MOSCA, SR.

ANGELO MOSCA, SR., IS BIG, bad, mean, and nasty! Make no mistake about that. The 305-pound Canadian won't, you can be sure.

Winning is the specialty of this brute, no matter how or against whom. Everything he accomplishes, every move he makes, every body he breaks, is for one person and one person alone—himself. He glories in the fact that he is accountable to no one but himself, a self-cen-tered whirlwind with destruction written all over him.

Still, the man who accounts to no one has a manager, one J. J. Dillon. It was Dillon who was responsible for bringing Mosca to the South. There the public was led to believe that Mosca was serving as the unofficial enforcer for the diabolical Kevin Sullivan and the Purple Haze. Nevertheless, he denies this vehemently. He is his own man, and damned be unto him who suggests otherwise.

Mosca was sensational in the South, tearing through everything and everyone with a death-and-destruction campaign. It was a campaign he took on tour on numerous occasions, winning titles, awards, trophies, and a substantial amount of money for his efforts.

Although he is mean and nasty, Mosca prides himself on being, in his own words, "the best wrestler in the world." Several who have doubted that in the ring have been made to pay for their lack of respect, Mosca believing that his opponents wouldn't emerge all bruised and bloodied if "they knew what they were doing."

But it isn't only those in the ring who feel the wrath of Mosca, Sr. During one of his stops on the East Coast Angelo became involved in a feud with wrestler-commentator Pat Patterson. At an interview Mosca availed himself of a metal pitcher laying near-at-hand and used it to pound home one of his points, viciously beating Patterson over the head. Needless to say, Mosca felt that the announcer "got exactly what he deserved."

That is Angelo Mosca, Sr., at one and the same time one of the best around today. And, one of the worst!

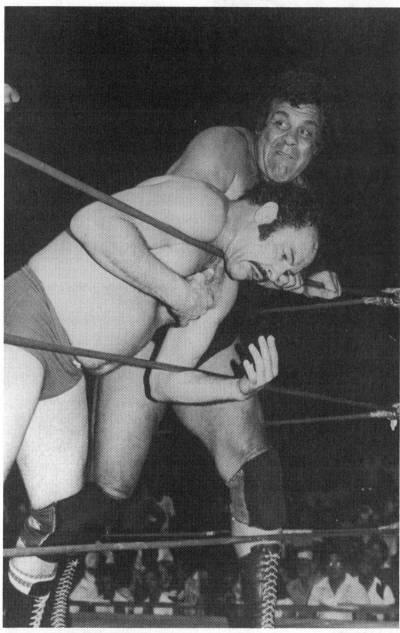

Mosca, Sr., teaches Tommy Gilbert the ropes.

Angelo Mosca, Sr., has a headlock on Ivan Putski.

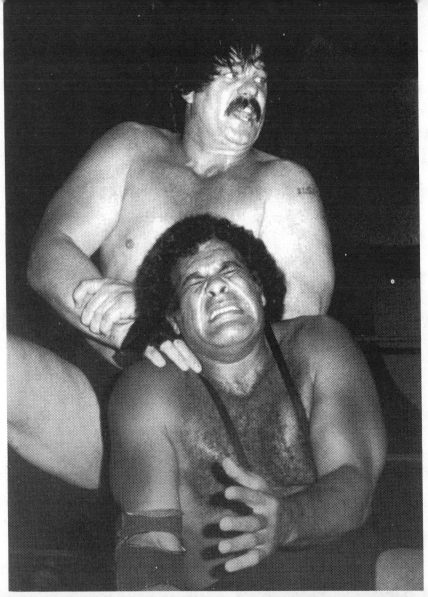

BLACK JACK MULLIGAN IS A man as big as all outdoors, which isn't surprising, considering that he comes from Eagle Pass, Texas, where he lives on a 150-acre ranch.

One of the biggest and most violent wrestlers ever to emerge from the great state of Texas, Black Jack Mulligan conjures up images of a raging cattle stampede or a locomotive out of control. Since leaving professional football back in 1968 Mulligan has been tackling some of the greatest names in the professional wrestling world, and has become a force to be reckoned with.

Awards always have been a way of life for Mulligan. At Eagle Pass High School he was all-city in football and wrestling,

Mulligan gives Angelo Mosca, Sr., an offer he can't refuse.

Andre the Giant gets a Black Jack from Mulligan.

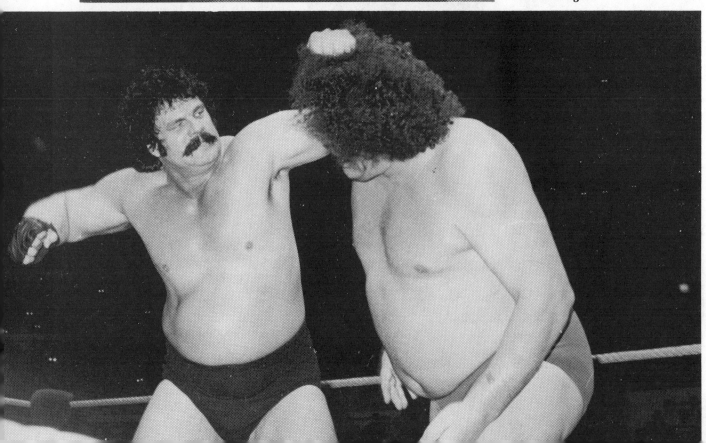

BLACK JACK MULLIGAN

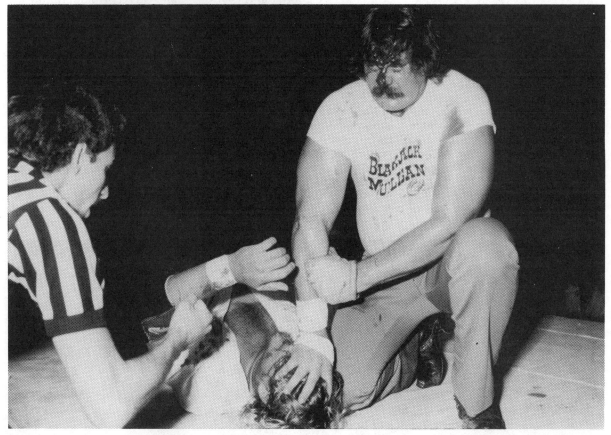

Black Jack Mulligan impresses Bobby Duncum.

and also starred in track and field. Although many colleges sought the highly talented Mulligan, Black Jack chose the University of Texas at El Paso to launch his career. During four years at UTEP he was selected as a Little College All-American for his feats in wrestling and football. After completing college, Black Jack was drafted by the Denver Broncos and played with both the Broncos and, later, the New York Jets.

A likable laid-back type, Mulligan can disarm you with his charming and affable personality, having a soft spot for children, animals, and friends. But once he steps into the ring, his "office," he is a master of utter mayhem. This dual approach to

life and profession comes from the fact that violence was a part of Black Jack's upbringing. As a child of nine, Mulligan was so much bigger than other kids that they ridiculed him in that cruel manner kids have. He solved the problem—and quieted his tormentors—by making it clear that he was not one to be laughed at, but rather someone to be feared. Black Jack will admit that his "mean streak" has always been a part of him. He can control it at times—but only outside the ring!

A throwback to days gone by when "men were men and women were damned glad of it," Mulligan exhibits a type of meanness in the ring that has been unseen for years, but one

he sees as a testing of the elasticity of the rules while never quite breaking them.

Even though Mulligan has won many titles and attained many of wrestling's greatest honors, he has no intentions of retiring. "Once you have made it to the top, you want to stay at the top," he asserts emphatically. He is not afraid of wrestling the best in the world, even looks forward to it, viewing each competitor as but another personal Everest. Black Jack would never, ever back down from a challenge. This is but one of the many reasons why Black Jack Mulligan is one in a million, a man who is proud of himself and proud of his accomplishments.

ONE MAN GANG

A CROSS BETWEEN AN OVER-weight Tarzan and Charles Manson, this awesome piece of timber is one man who is definitely not easy to forget. Tipping the scales at 450 pounds, this 6-foot 6-inch wild man paints an imposing picture as he enters the ring, swinging his chains, animal skins draping his huge frame. Very few have dared to mess with the mammoth One Man Gang on his climb to the top of the wrestling heap.

Says good buddy J. J. Dillon of the Gang, ''He's my kind of people. I only associate with the best, and I've got to put the One Man Gang in that category. Just look at the man, and you'll see what I mean . . . they just don't come much tougher. He's got a mean streak that runs from the top of his scalp to the tip of his toes.''

The One Man Gang began his career in Kentucky, and in his travels he has been associated with such diabolical men as Scandor Akbar, Sir Oliver Humperdink, and J. J. Dillon. Each one of these infamous managers saw—and rightly so—the makings of a champion.

Sir Oliver Humperdink was the one man most instrumental in taking the One Man Gang out of the preliminaries and getting him into the main events. Although the Gang always had the drive needed to succeed, it took Humperdink to bring it to the surface. Says the Gang of his first manager, ''He came to me when I really needed guidance and direction and taught me quite a few tricks. That Hump is quite a character, and we got along quite well. Thanks to my ability and his wisdom, I made it. But today I don't need him or

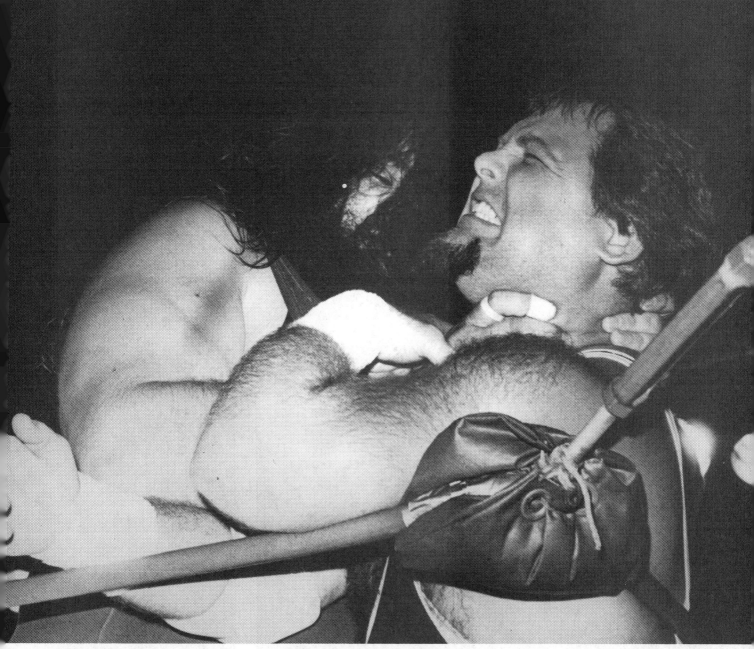

Opposite: One Man Gang gets Jerry Lawler's attention—and then some. Above: Lawler is choked up with emotion at the sight of One Man Gang.

anyone else, because I can make it on my own.''

During 1983 the One Man Gang controlled the Mid-Atlantic area, waging numerous wars against the ''Boogie Woogie Man'' Jimmy Valiant and Joe Le-Duc. Then the Gang toured Japan, and finally returned to the States and Florida.

When the Gang first arrived in the Sunshine State, ''Gentleman'' Jim Holiday served as his adviser. But then the Gang sided with Ron Bass and J. J. Dillon. It has taken Dillon just one look at this huge man to realize who he wanted on his side.

Perhaps the most disturbing incident as far as the Florida fans were concerned occurred in Tampa when Barry Windham battled Ron Bass for the prized saddle. The One Man Gang waited quietly behind the dressing-room door for a chance to ambush Barry Windham. Windham finally managed to pin Bass, but as he turned to claim the saddle, the Gang, joined by Bass, jumped him from behind. They humiliated him by putting the saddle on his back. The fans were livid.

After this incident, Black Jack Mulligan joined Windham in revenge, and soon it was open warfare between Mulligan and the Gang. The two battled all over the country, making World War II look tame. But that is all in the past. Not too long ago the Gang had a change of heart and joined Dusty Rhodes's ''Family.'' But will the awesome One Man Gang be content wrestling alongside former enemies Black Jack Mulligan, Barry Windham, and Rhodes? It's not likely.

Feuds and fury alike, the One Man Gang has definitely made a name for himself in the arenas of the world—a big name.

"POLISH POWER" IVAN PUTSKI has simply done it all. Originally from Krakow, Poland, Putski has built himself into one of the premier stars on the wrestling scene.

For the past fifteen years Ivan Putski has dominated the sport with his charismatic charm and phenomenal strength. Although not blessed with the refined

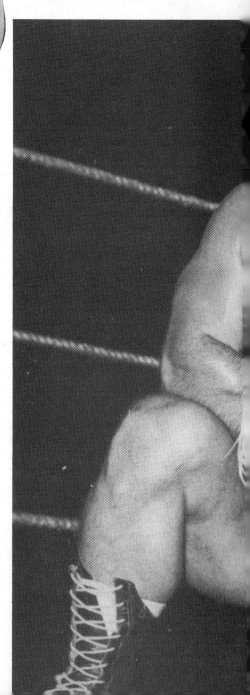

Above: "Polish power" as demonstrated by the prince of power, Ivan Putski. Right: Putski shows "Superstar" Billy Graham his idea of "solidarity."

IVAN PUTSKI

skills of a Bob Backlund, Putski has more than made up for any lack of skills by his fierce determination and the loyal support of his "Polish army." "The General," as Putski is affectionately referred to, is loved by everyone. "The fans mean a lot to me," he says. "Without their support I wouldn't be in the position I am today."

Over the years Putski has met and defeated all of the big stars in the sport. Men such as "Superstar" Billy Graham, Ken Patera, Ivan Koloff, Mr. Fuji, Stan Hansen, Paul Orndorff, the Magnificent Muraco, and many others have met defeat at the hands of the great Polish sensation.

Besides being an excellent singles wrestler, Putski is also a master in tag team competition. In October 1979 Putski, along with Tito Santana, captured the WWF tag team title from Jerry and Johnny Valiant; Ivan also has twice held tag team titles in Texas. It seems that Ivan Putski has always been a winner. Like a fine wine, Ivan Putski just gets better with age.

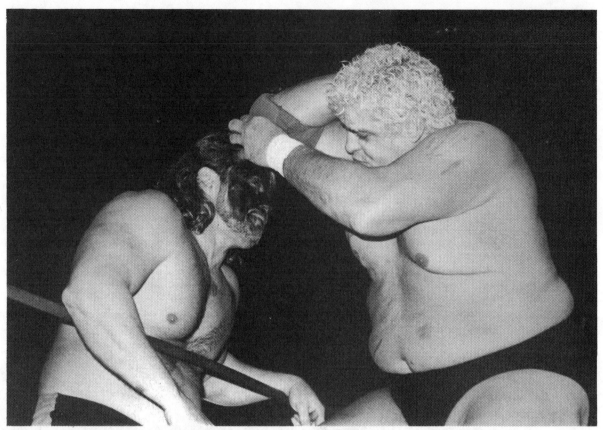

The "bionic elbow" of Rhodes plays devil with the face of the satanical Kevin Sullivan.

Rhodes with his famed chinlock on the famed chin of Ivan Koloff.

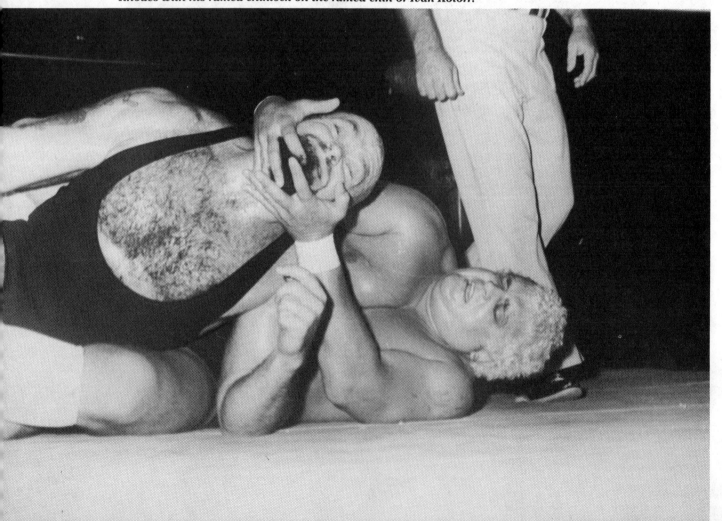

DUSTY RHODES

PERHAPS THE MOST RECOGnizable, if not the most complex, man in the sport has to be "the American Dream." With his unmistakable blond curls and ample physique, Dusty Rhodes has garnered a reputation among his fans that is second to none. Since his debut in November 1969 there have been few fans who have not known of Dusty Rhodes.

Dusty's achievements in the sport are awesome. He has held dozens of singles and tag team championship titles, including the Florida heavyweight, the Southern heavyweight, the Mid-Atlantic, the Georgia heavyweight, the US tag team, and the NWA tag team titles. He is a two-time NWA world heavyweight champion, having defeated Harley Race twice to capture that crown—his first reign in August 1979 lasted only five days; his second title reign was from June 21, 1981, until September 17, 1981.

He is filled with overwhelming enthusiasm, and his extroverted style of mixing seriousness with jive has endeared him to thousands of fans throughout the world. There is only one American Dream, one man who, deep in his heart, is happy with his life. That is a rare quality to find in any man, and Dusty Rhodes is the rarest of them all.

Dusty Rhodes with his NWA world title belt during his reign as champion.

TOMMY RICH

"WILDFIRE" TOMMY RICH was one half of the New Fabulous Ones. He is one of the most dedicated, polite, and considerate wrestlers ever to grace the ring. Also, as befits someone who is still called Fabulous, he is one of the most skilled.

During his early years in Tennessee Rich wrestled as part of a tag team with Jackie Fargo, the force behind the New Fabs. Then, on April 27, 1981, he successfully captured the NWA world heavyweight title in a match with Harley Race. But, as fate would have it, in a rematch only four days later, in a heart-breaking moment, he lost the title back to Race.

Tommy picked up the pieces and tried to sort out his confusion. A long-standing feud with Buzz Sawyer became so much a part of him, a growing obsession, that it almost destroyed him. Eventually, however, the two came to terms with each other, and Tommy made peace with himself as well, now able to concentrate on his career.

His is a career that was built on success and promises more. What else could you expect from a man like Rich, someone nicknamed the Fabulous One?

Rich gets the Masked Superstar in an abdominal stretch.

Tommy treats Ole Anderson to a Rich headlock.

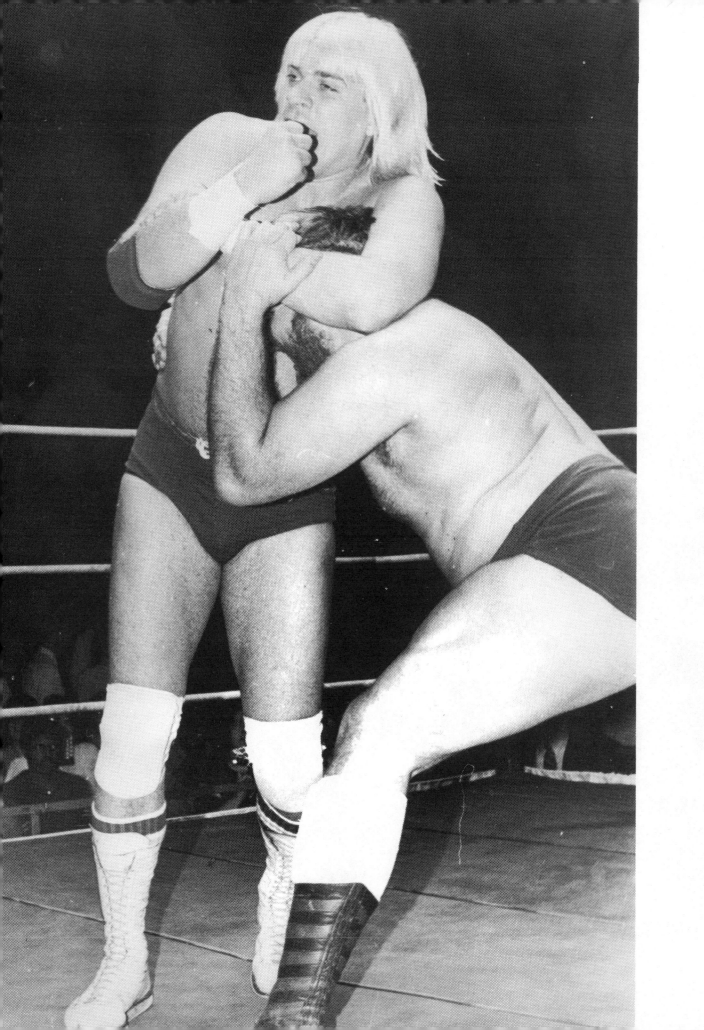

MIKE ROTUNDO

THE 1980'S HAVE PRODUCED many new young superstars in wrestling, but one of the most promising is Mike Rotundo. This handsome young Italian has come a long way in a very short time, and the best is yet to come.

Mike became involved in wrestling at an early age. Always interested in athletics, he learned the basics of the sport and then took his knowledge to Syracuse University, where he excelled on the mat, winning the Eastern championship.

He had been active in football, as well as wrestling, in college, but after he finished school, Mike went on to train for several months to prepare for a wrestling career. His first professional exposure came at a tournament in Germany. The young Rotundo competed against men from all over the world, and this international service was just what he needed to get him on the right track as a pro.

When he returned from the tournament, he began wrestling in Canada. He eventually gravitated to the Mid-Atlantic area, where he captured the Mid-Atlantic TV title, but his reign was short-lived when Dick Slater upended the likable young star.

But that was merely a television title, and Rotundo moved to Florida to take on new challenges and to rule the South. "To capture the Southern title after only a month in the area is something I never expected to happen," says the modest Rotundo. "I came to Florida hoping to show the people my moves, my style, and eventually after I had established my credentials, I hoped I would get a chance at the crown." Well, that chance came a lot sooner than Mike, or anyone else, expected, but when it came, he was ready. This was the opportunity he had been waiting for since he was 12 years old.

Mike had worked hard while in the Mid-Atlantic area, and obviously his hard work paid off. He learned various holds, moves, and maneuvers from the Mid-Atlantic's best, including Jay Youngblood and Roddy Piper, as well as workout routines from Ricky Steamboat. The determined young Italian never missed a workout and claims, "If I've learned anything at all in my life, it's that nothing comes easy. I've always been instilled with the philosophy that success comes to those who work for it, and I've made it a point to strive for success my whole life."

At 6 feet 2 inches, 240 pounds, Mike Rotundo is in superb condition. But he admits that he still has a lot to learn. Does he have the ingredients necessary to rise to the top? Judging from his determination, strength, and ability, one can confidently say yes.

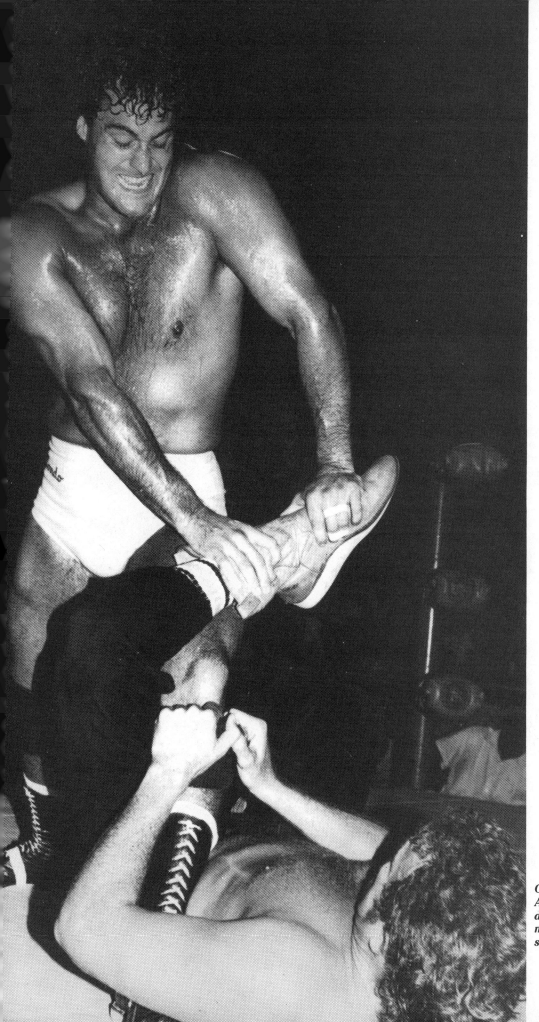

Opposite: Mike Rotundo has Angelo Mosca, Sr., caught in an abdominal stretch. Left: Rotundo makes Jake Roberts into his own special version of a snake.

71

TITO SANTANA

TITO SANTANA'S RISE TO fame is one of wrestling's most recent legends. In his six plus years of wrestling this exciting and talented young grappler from Mexico has managed not only to win the WWF Intercontinental title but also to win such events as the West Texas tag team championship (with good friend Ted DiBiase) and the WWF tag team championship (with Ivan Putski). Although he began his career wrestling in tag teams, Santana is now competing exclusively in single bouts, and is doing extremely well. But then again Tito Santana has always done well. In addition to his strength, stamina, and skill, he is also a decent sportsman who always tries to respect the rules.

Watching Tito in the ring, it is obvious that he has learned his lessons perfectly. He is well versed in every scientific hold and technique imaginable and can also execute a wide assortment of aerial maneuvers. Tito is truly dedicated to the sport—and by day he can be found in a gymnasium somewhere, readying himself for his next match.

Like many wrestlers, Tito Santana played professional football for two years before joining the wrestling ranks. In 1975, after graduating from college, Santana joined the Kansas City Chiefs for one season. In 1976 he played in Vancouver, British Columbia, in the Canadian Football League for the BC Lions. After that he tried his hand at professional wrestling, and his football days were over.

In 1983, while wrestling in the AWA, Tito had the opportunity to team up with the talented Rick Martel. Unfortunately, the partnership did not last long, for Santana was already committed to go on to Atlanta before the two had even thought of teaming up together. But for six weeks Santana and Martel traveled everywhere and hit it off tremendously. The fans were behind them 100 percent, and their styles complemented each other's perfectly. As a team they were simply fantastic, and now both are champions.

As WWF Intercontinental champion, Tito Santana has met and defeated all the top men in the profession, including former champion the Magnificent Muraco, Paul "Mr. Wonderful" Orndorff, David Schultz, Mike Sharpe, and others. Although Santana is an excellent wrestler, life at the top is not easy. He is constantly pursued by the best wrestlers in the sport and will invariably fall from the pinnacle someday. But the likable Latin with the fiery disposition will be on or near the top for many years to come.

Tito Santana gets ahead of Wild Samoan Afa.

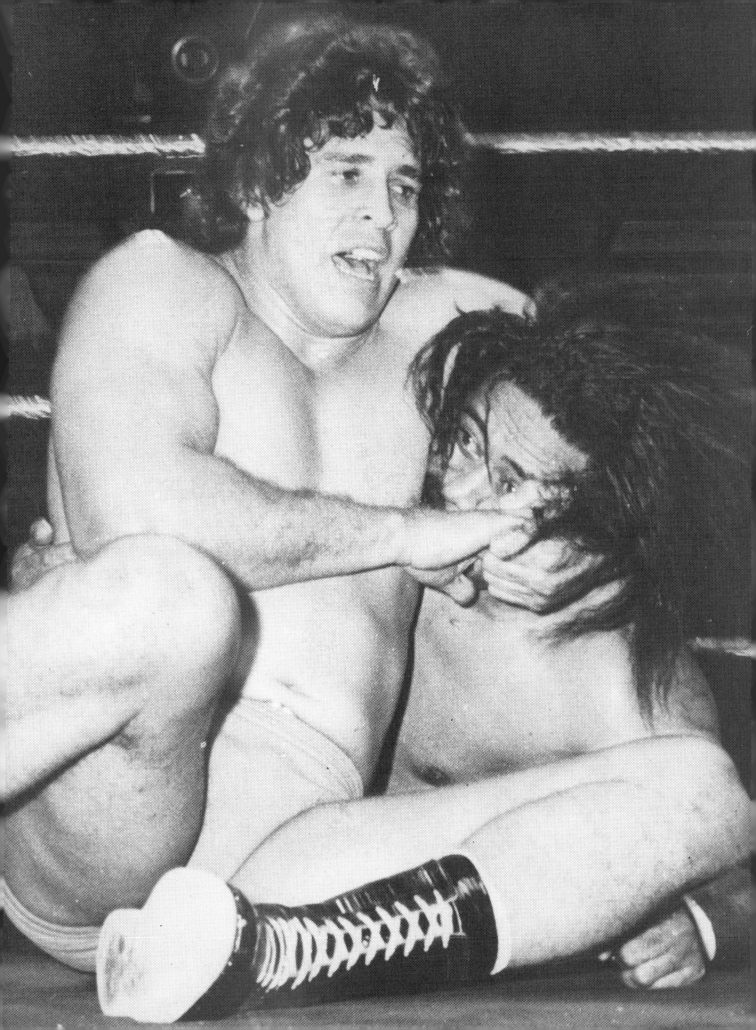

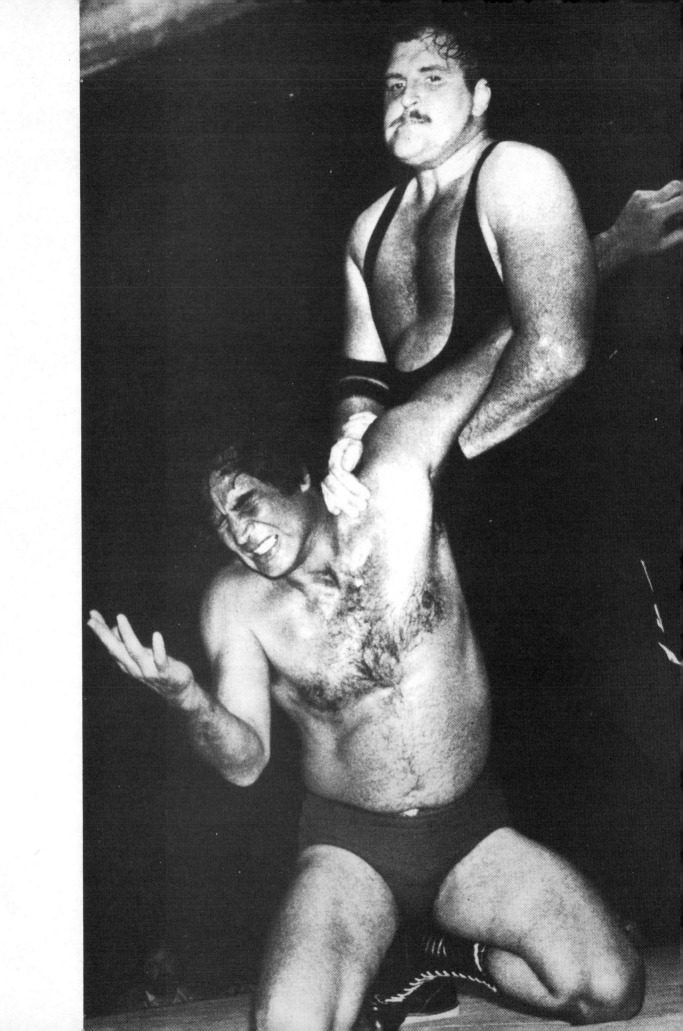

SERGEANT SLAUGHTER

WITH A FAIR NUMBER OF EXtremely large, tough, and driven men in professional wrestling, what is it that sets certain individuals apart? And what is it that gets the fans behind a wrestler 100 percent, pushing him up the ladder from a mere great to one of the elite? In the case of Sergeant Slaughter it's the love of God and country, the "death-before-dishonor" drive, and an intense hatred for America's enemies and detractors that have made him one of the most respected men in wrestling. And one of its great superheroes, as well.

Like the stereotypical drill sergeant shown in the movies, Slaughter was first received with an apprehensive fear. Fans referred to him as Gomer and hated everything about him. But more recently he has earned the respect of fans and foes alike, and has, in true Hollywood fashion, come to be loved. This is not to say that love and respect came easily to this hard, distant man, a man many feel began the downfall of former champion Bob Backlund. Still, the Sergeant is now a big favorite of the fans. And this radical transformation is as interesting as it is incredible to believe.

Perhaps it all started on that fateful evening when Iranian "students" overran the Marines at the US embassy in Tehran and took American citizens as hostages. It was an unconscienable act, one that did not sit well with the Sergeant or with his patriotic beliefs.

The ramifications of this international act of terrorism were never far from the thoughts of the ex-Marine. When, just after the death of Slaughter's guiding force, the Grand Wizard, Fred Blassie imported Iran's Iron Sheik, who subsequently beat Backlund and

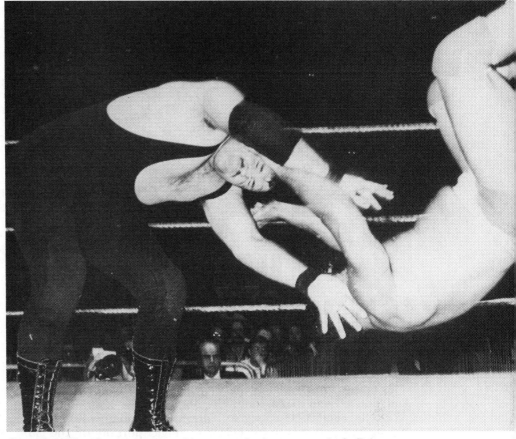

Opposite: The Sergeant gives his manual of arms to Jack Brisco. Above: Sergeant Slaughter, with his own special brand of combat, gives Pedro Morales an eyes—and limbs—right.

used his new title to make pro-Iranian and anti-American statements, Slaughter became a Marine possessed. The Sergeant's *semper fi* Marine ideology finally had an outlet for its full expression. Even after Hulk Hogan won the belt from the Iron Sheik, Slaughter's sights were still set on "this open sore on the face of Uncle Sam."

Several times the two have locked horns in mortal combat, each contest more brutal than the previous one. Many feel that future battles with the Iron Sheik will be even more savage, perhaps rivaling the most fierce in the history of the sport. The danger is that when they're finally over, neither man will be in condition, mentally or physically, ever to wrestle again.

The Sergeant's goal, simply stated, is: "I want that so-called Ayatolla Blassie and his Iranian maggot as well as all the other detractors from this great country beaten out of the ring—and out of the country. If this ends my career as a wrestler, I'll leave the ring a happy man."

The Sergeant's future aside, he is now a changed man and fights a never-ending battle in the name of truth, justice, and the all-American way. So, call him sir, call him Sarge, but never, never call him the ultimate insult to any Marine: Gomer. *Sarge,* we salute you, a real American patriot!

Left: Superfly with ex-manager "Captain" Lou Albano, a onetime ferocious duo. Opposite: Superfly is a bloody mess after being attacked by Albano and Ray Stevens.

JIMMY "SUPERFLY" SNUKA

STRENGTH, SIZE, AGILITY, drive, and incredible natural talent—such are the ingredients of wrestling's great champions. And no one can claim Jimmy "Superfly" Snuka is lacking in any of these essential elements to wrestling grandeur.

The Superfly is also an extremely relaxed and kind man outside the ring, and one of the most popular wrestlers in the world today. His is a story of victory and happiness, right? The answer that echoes throughout arenas across the country is no!—not if his archenemy, "Captain" Lou Albano, can help it.

Jimmy hails from the Fiji Islands of the South Pacific. And his laid-back charm proves that the Islands are an essential part of this man. Still, the desire for competition is also a big part of Snuka. This desire brought him to the United States and, coupled with astonishing talent, helped him to win the US heavyweight, Pacific Northwest heavyweight, and the NWA world tag team belts. However, the lure of fame and fortune brought Jimmy to the WWF area. But it was Lou Albano who stood between Jimmy and his dream and who now leads us to the tragic portion of the Superfly's career.

For a while Jimmy was in New York, finding the Big Apple to his taste, and soon he was a main attraction under Albano's guidance. Then, Jimmy underwent a tremendous change: he ignored Albano's rule-breaking game plan and began following the scientific school of wrestling, and winning because of it. This didn't sit well with a man as pompous and egotistical as Albano, and violent dressing-room clashes between the two became common. The pressure between these very different personalities finally erupted on former champion Buddy Rogers's television show, *Rogers's Corner,* and spewed over like Mt. Helena.

Rogers had found out that Lou Albano was not legally Snuka's manager, but Jimmy's trusting nature had led him to believe that he was. Furthermore, Rogers also discovered that Jimmy had never received one cent he had earned under the conscienceless Albano. Furious, Albano wisely left the set, fearful of his safety, while Jimmy and Rogers quickly became friends. And a team. Yet, Albano wasn't through with his cheating ways and began attacking Snuka. With the help of Fred Blassie and Ray "Crippler" Stevens, a plot was hatched: as Jimmy and Stevens prepared for a match, Blassie and Albano joined in, mercilessly beating Snuka until he lay splattered with blood outside the ring.

Few will ever forget the revenge gained by Jimmy for this unprincipled act. The Superfly and Albano clashed in a packed Madison Square Garden, with Jimmy sending his unscrupulous ex-manager fleeing like a wounded dog, nursing his wounds. Still, for months, as Albano put it, "Snuka hated me with such a passion that he'd sign on to wrestle any of my men. Meanwhile, with my carefully thought out plan, I knew that he would never get a shot at the WWF title. By chasing me I've kept him from his dream. See what happens when you desert the Captain?"

When Snuka heard of Albano's nasty diatribe, he replied, "Brother, I've learned a lot. You tell me to forget Albano? There's a deep hurt inside me that will never die. But, like I say, I did learn a lot, and I promise my fans the Superfly will fly to even greater heights."

With Lou Albano now a part of his past, and with the fans behind him all the way, who can doubt that Jimmy "Superfly" Snuka will finally realize his dream? He deserves it!

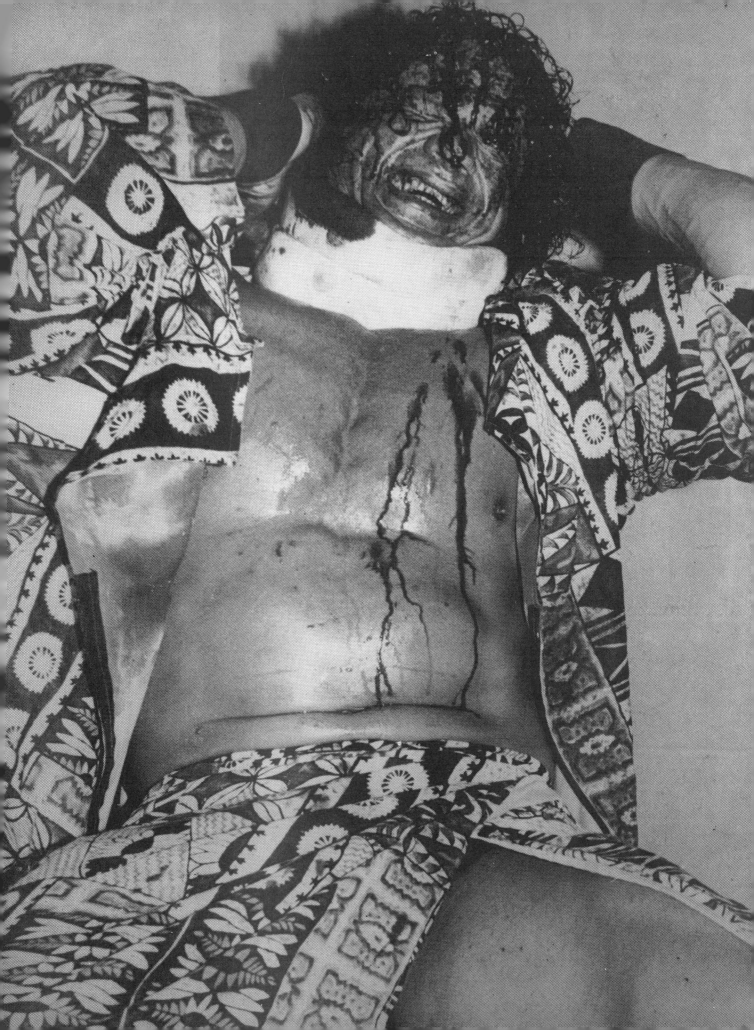

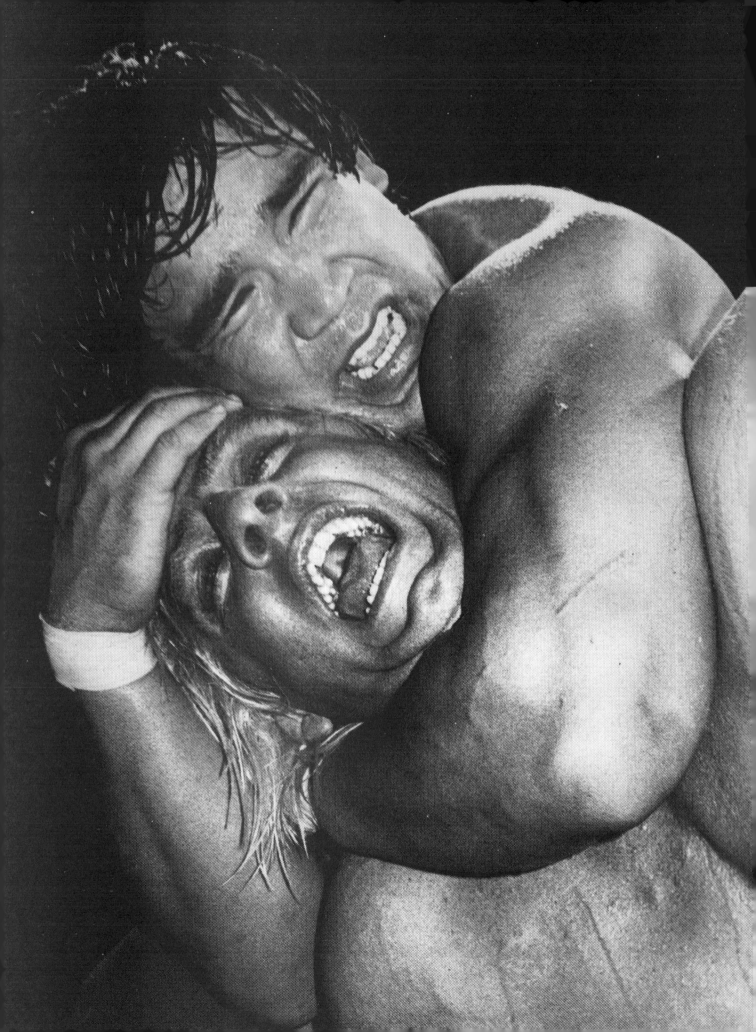

RICK STEAMBOAT

RICK STEAMBOAT IS A CLEAN, gifted, scientific wrestler with a solid sense of sportsmanship who can face any challenge and handle the most brutal components. In a very short span of time this young man from Honolulu, Hawaii, has gone from being a highly regarded rookie—he was named Rookie of the Year by the fans in 1977—to one of the true superstars of the sport.

Steamboat uses his knowledge of karate, along with his wrestling skills, to make himself an exceptional fighter. At 232 pounds and in top condition, this younger grappler continually amazes his doting fans with his versatility. His abdominal stretch is one of his more well-known moves, but he hates to rely on just one hold and changes them frequently to keep his opponents on guard at all times. He has a move called the double thrust that he is fond of using and also uses a lot of back kicks, back fists, and dive splashes or double chops.

Steamboat frequently changes his style of wrestling according to his opponent, and this is perhaps his greatest attribute as a wrestler. He has entered the ring with quite a number of very different wrestlers—Ric Flair, Greg Valentine, Baron Von Raschke, and Black Jack Mulligan—and has dealt with them all individually. And individually they have all felt the sting of his attacks.

In the past he has had some brutal clashes with Ric Flair, when they were both fighting for the US heavyweight championship. Flair once threw Steamboat on the floor, ground his face into the cement, then took his belt and ground that into his face as well. Steamboat had a badly discolored face for quite a long time after that, and blurred vision in one eye.

Opposite: Rick Steamboat applies a headlock to the blond locks of Ric Flair. Above: Steamboat has Jimmy "Superfly" Snuka at his mercy with an armlock.

At one point Ricky Steamboat lost his desire and drive and announced his retirement. He claimed that he needed a change of scenery, and so he opened his own gym, where he did nothing but work out every day—far from the mad(en)ing crowd of wrestling. But after a while that old rassling bug bit the Happy Hawaiian again, and Steamboat returned to the ring.

Needless to say, his fans were ecstatic, and just as anxious as he for him to win the world championship. It is inevitable that he and Flair will meet again, and then the true champion will emerge.

"CHIEF" JAY STRONGBOW

HE'S FROM PAWHUSKA, OKLA-homa, and he's one of the fans' most popular wrestlers. That's right, he's Chief Jay Strongbow. For over 15 years his popularity has grown to the point where it has now reached unprece-dented heights.

The Chief is always colorful. Dressed in authentic Indian re-galia, he performs his thrilling war dance before each and ev-ery bout—a dance that almost has become as much a part of the wrestling scene as Chief Jay Strongbow himself. But it's not his war dance that has made the Chief colorful, it's his Indian holds: his tomahawk chops, patented knee lifts, and famous Indian sleeper hold. Slipping through the grip of his oppo-nents, the Chief can knock them silly with any of them. No won-der the Chief has so many de-voted followers!

Strongbow's immense popu-larity has grown over time. Part of the reason is that he returns all the warmth and adoration he receives from his fans. His will-ingness to accommodate his le-gions of followers is legendary. At arenas throughout the world he is always signing autographs and, when possible, posing for pictures. Adults, promoters, and children all love this au-thentic hero.

Strongbow believes that part of his mass appeal stems from the fact that he dances with his heart. He feels that the fans trust him, and determined never to betray that trust, he puts his heart and soul into his wres-tling.

The Chief hit the top of the profession in its golden years, from 1970 to 1978, during the championship reigns of Bruno Sammartino and Pedro Mor-ales, and even, incredible as it sounds, surpassed both of those great heroes in popularity. More

"Chief" Jay and Jules Strongbow hold up their WWF tag team title belts.

importantly, he was the out-standing contender during those years—anyone who wanted a ti-tle match having to get by Strongbow. The Chief also held two championship titles during this period, both were WWF world tag team titles, the first with Sonny King in 1972, the second with Chief Billy White Wolf in 1977.

Strongbow has teamed with many of the world's great wres-tlers and remembers those times nostalgically. But, there were less pleasant days for the Chief. Lou Albano touched off a deep rivalry with Strongbow, Al-bano's terror tactics injuring Strongbow illegally several times. His dislike of Albano comes naturally, the manager having pestered Strongbow to be managed by him also. But Strongbow would have nothing to do with Albano or his tactics: he gave him a resounding no to his ever-present request. Since then Albano has tried to make life hell for the Chief.

The last regular partner the Chief had was his own brother, Jules. Their collective target was Mr. Fuji and Mr. Saito, the WWF tag team champs. At their match at Madison Square Gar-den, Jules and Jay ostensibly won the belt from Fuji and Saito. But the victory was not to be, as Strongbow's antagonist, Lou Albano, now serving as manager of Fuji and Saito, held that Fuji's foot was over the

bottom rope at the count of three—and his appeal was up-held.

A rematch was scheduled. And, after a wild struggle, Fuji and Saito emerged victorious. But they achieved their so-called "victory" only by using a foreign substance, salt, to blind Jules. After several months of bitter warfare Jay and Jules again regained the belt. But shortly thereafter they lost it to the Wild Samoans.

Feeling that the twosome had lost some of their "magic," the two decided to split up. But on his own or as part of a team, Chief Jay Strongbow has a gift that excites and inspires his fans.

Chief Jay Strongbow clamps a sleeper hold on Mr. X.

81

"JUMBO" TOMMY TSURUTA

"JUMBO" TOMMY TSURUTA has been wrestling professionally since October 31, 1972. Prior to turning professional, Tsuruta was an outstanding amateur wrestler and represented Japan in the 1972 Olympic Games in Munich, Germany.

While just a boy, Tsuruta's dream was to grow up to become a professional wrestler just like his boyhood idol, the Giant Baba. When Tsuruta was in college, he had the opportunity to meet Baba, and was told to pursue his goal with all his heart and soul. After the Olympics were history, Tsuruta approached the Giant Baba once again, hoping to turn professional. For three months the great Baba took Tsuruta under his wing and worked with him every day. He taught young Tsuruta the difference in style between professional wrestling and amateur wrestling. After Tsuruta had absorbed Baba's teachings, he was sent to Amarillo, Texas, where he then trained under the watchful eyes of Dory and Terry Funk.

Tsuruta trained very hard, and he was an adept student. In time he learned the scientific maneuvers of Dory Funk as well as the roughhouse tactics of brother Terry. He was then ready for his first professional match in Amarillo. In his first bout there, before his hometown fans, Tsuruta defeated Moose Morowski—his professional career was truly launched. He stayed in western Texas for several more months, however, before finally returning to his home in Japan.

During his professional career Tsuruta has held the United States title, the International title, and the International tag team title with his old hero, the Giant Baba. He holds victories over many of today's superstars, including Dory Funk, Jr.;

Opposite: Jumbo has Jimmy Snuka right where he wants him. Above: Tsuruta proudly displays his AWA world championship belt.

Billy Robinson; Wahoo McDaniel; Harley Race; Terry Funk; Abdullah the Butcher; Jack Brisco; Ric Flair; and Mil Mascaras. Tsuruta has battled for the NWA title on several occasions. Although he has come extremely close to winning it, it has eluded him.

He stunned the wrestling world, however, with his 32-minute victory over Nick Bockwinkel to win the ever-prestigious AWA title on February 23, 1984. When he went into the championship battle, few people thought he had much of a chance against the well-seasoned Bockwinkel. But Tsuruta pulled it off, and in so doing put his name in the record books.

To prove that his victory over

Bockwinkel wasn't just a fluke, the two met again three days later in Osaka, Japan. They were both counted out in a wild and uncontrollable brawl, but the next day Bockwinkel left Japan and headed for the States—without his cherished AWA gold belt.

Jumbo Tsuruta held the prestigious AWA title for three months, defending it all over the world against many worthy competitors. Unfortunately, on May 13, 1984, in the St. Paul Civic Center, Tsuruta lost the title to Rick Martel. Already in his young career, Tsuruta has held one of the highest honors in his sport. With his talent, the Japanese sensation should someday achieve the pinnacle of success once again.

JIMMY VALIANT

THE FEARLESS BOOGIE WOO-gie Man from the streets of New York City is one of the sport's star attractions. Wherever he appears he is loved by one and all! Down South, in the Mid-Atlantic area, where he is worshiped, fans flock to arenas to see him, to cheer him on, and to be part of the "Jimmy Valiant experience."

When Jimmy rocks and rolls his way down the aisle and into an arena, fans go crazy. His appearance is like a giant happening right out of the 1960's, a great love-in celebrating peace and happiness. Jimmy has kept that lovin' feeling of the sixties alive throughout the wrestling world—that is, until he steps into the ring. Then he becomes a wild man.

Once inside the ring, Jimmy charges his opponent and attacks relentlessly. He will not give up until his opponent has been beaten into submission. "Growing up in the streets of the Big Apple I learned how to survive, and that's what I do when I step through these ropes. God forbid you should dare to cross me, because I don't just get mad—I get even," says the Boogie Woogie Man.

"I advocate peace, love, and togetherness. That's the real me you see walking the streets and singing on the corners every day. Then there's my dark side," Valiant admits. "Once you cross me, Daddy, then my other side takes over. There's good and bad in everyone; but I live for the good. Once you've destroyed my goodness, then there's nothing left for me to do but get downright nasty."

Some of the wrestlers who have caused Jimmy to "get downright nasty" include Gary Hart, the Great Kabuki, and Paul Jones and his Assassins. The Hart-Kabuki duo blinded Valiant with fire, burned his eyes with Kabuki's mysterious green mist, and broke his favorite tape recorder. Says Valiant of Kabuki, "He's taken me to the limit. When I know I'm going to face him, then, Daddy, be prepared for war! You've got to hurt the man before he hurts you. It took a while before my eyes healed, and I still can't see too well out of them. Hey, it's hard not being able to see all those southern belles the way I used to, and it gets me mad, Daddy, knowing it's all Kabuki's fault. He'll pay. And Hart, too!"

The war between Valiant and Kabuki has progressed to the point where there can be only one champion in the South. And the fans are betting on that one champ being "that boy from New York City." As for the Assassins, the villainous masked duo, with their conniving manager Paul Jones, attacked Valiant one day and cut off his beard. Valiant vowed revenge, and once the smoke had cleared was able to unmask the Assassins.

During some of his most famous bouts Jimmy has taken on—and beaten—such stars as Ivan Koloff, Sergeant Slaughter, Don Kernodle, Joe LeDuc, Jake "the Snake" Roberts, the One Man Gang, the Magic Dragon, and many others. "When I first got my act together, Sir Oliver Humperdink showed up and tried to take over," recalls Valiant. But Valiant took care of Humperdink instead—and everybody else he brought in to help.

However, no story about Jimmy Valiant would be complete without mentioning his brothers, Luscious Johnny and Gentleman Jerry. Before Jimmy's mass appeal, he and his brothers were despised everywhere they wrestled. Early in his career Jimmy formed a highly successful tag team with his brother Johnny. Together the Valiants captured titles all over the world—successfully campaigning in the Midwest as well as in the WWF area. Soon the two became a threesome, with Gentleman Jerry joining his brothers in creating havoc wherever they appeared.

After a successful run in the WWF, the brothers went their separate ways, with Jimmy ending up in Tennessee, where he altered his style and became an instant celebrity. His rise to the top was directly attributable to the groundwork he did in Tennessee. Today a love affair continues between the Boogie Woogie Man and his southern fans. The Yankee from New York City has made a big hit in the sunny South—one that should, like Old Man River, keep right on rollin' along.

Above: The Boogie Woogie Man digs the Great Kabuki—with Kabuki's own kendo stick. Opposite: Valiant has the abominable Kabuki in an abdominal stretch.

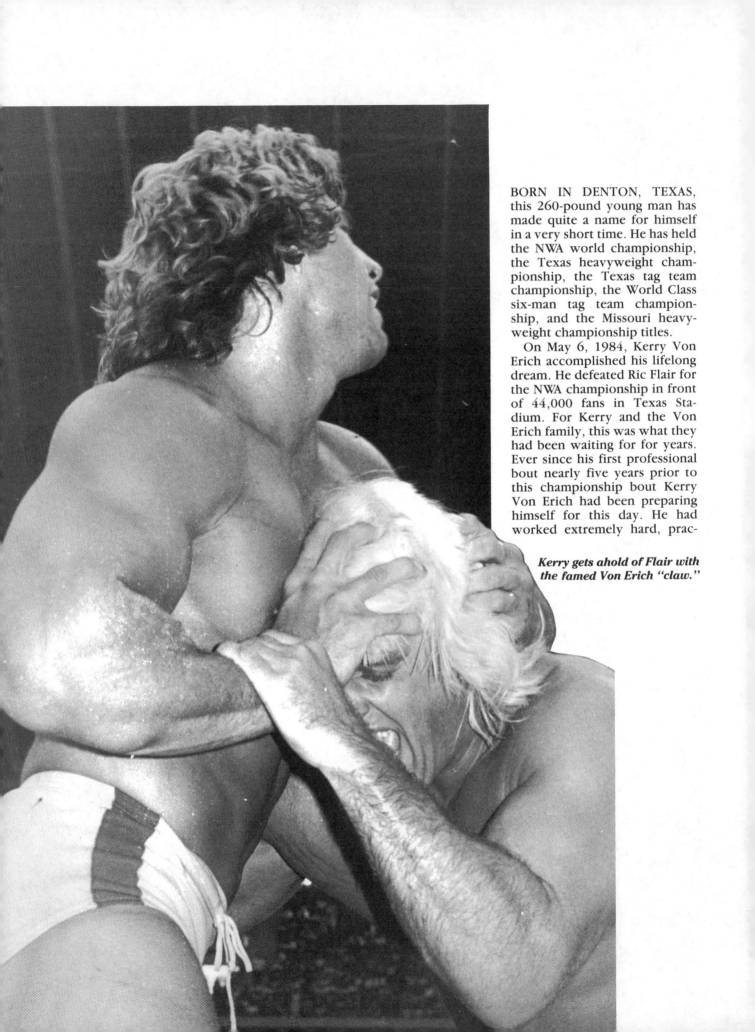

BORN IN DENTON, TEXAS, this 260-pound young man has made quite a name for himself in a very short time. He has held the NWA world championship, the Texas heavyweight championship, the Texas tag team championship, the World Class six-man tag team championship, and the Missouri heavyweight championship titles.

On May 6, 1984, Kerry Von Erich accomplished his lifelong dream. He defeated Ric Flair for the NWA championship in front of 44,000 fans in Texas Stadium. For Kerry and the Von Erich family, this was what they had been waiting for for years. Ever since his first professional bout nearly five years prior to this championship bout Kerry Von Erich had been preparing himself for this day. He had worked extremely hard, prac-

Kerry gets ahold of Flair with the famed Von Erich "claw."

KERRY VON ERICH

ticing for hours on end, ever faithful to his own rigorous routines. When Kerry stepped into the ring on May 6, he was ready.

It is not coincidental that long before the bout Kerry had repeatedly promised to win the championship for his brother, who had died an untimely death while on tour in Japan. In fact, it was David Von Erich who had been expected to win the title. The Von Erich family was understandably devastated by David's death, but his death also intensified Kerry's desire to make it to the top to honor his brother.

Unfortunately, Kerry's reign as champion did not last long. On May 24, 1984, while touring Japan, Kerry lost the belt back to former champion Ric Flair in a sensational battle that ended when Flair momentarily pulled Kerry's shoulders to the mat.

Kerry Von Erich held the NWA championship title for a total of 18 days. When asked what went wrong in Japan, Kerry said that nothing had gone wrong. He offered no alibis or excuses. His only regret was the strong feeling that he had let his family and friends down.

But at 24 years of age, Kerry Von Erich's career is just beginning. He is too talented not to wear the crown again. Kerry Von Erich has a bright future ahead of him, and with his determination and drive, there's no telling what he can do. The sky's the limit.

The Von Erich family in Texas Stadium: Fritz Von Erich, Mike Von Erich, Kevin Von Erich, Chris Von Erich, and Kerry Von Erich after winning the six-man tag team trophy.

KEVIN VON ERICH

Kevin with a Flair for a leglock.

and easily bounces back. Somehow, Flair managed to trip Kevin up: he lifted him off the mat and tossed him into the ropes. When the referee tried to step between the two wrestlers, he soon found himself lying outside the ring. Kevin then went flying over the top rope and landed on the hard cement floor. Flair proceeded to the outside of the ring and attempted to knock Von Erich into complete oblivion. But Kevin was prepared and knocked Flair hard as he approached. The two wrestlers then moved back into the ring, leaving the referee still immobilized outside the ring. Kevin then moved his offensive into full force and in grand style. He tossed the champion across the ring, and Flair flipped over the ropes and landed on the floor.

Another referee, David Manning, then rushed to ringside in an attempt to restore some order. Finally, Kevin sailed majestically through the air and landed squarely on Flair, who went down like a ton of bricks. Referee Manning counted to three, and Kevin thought he had won the championship.

A few moments later, though, referee Lubich managed to stumble back into the ring and take away the belt from the challenger. Unfortunately, the moment Kevin sailed over the top rope and out of the ring, Flair was automatically disqualified. It was a great disappointment for Von Erich.

Kevin took the loss with the grace of a great man. He believes that either he or his brother will somehow win the world title. There is no jealousy between the brothers. They are united in their quest to win the title for the Von Erich family, and their late brother, David.

KEVIN VON ERICH IS UNIQUE, but he is not one of a kind. He is the oldest son of the great Fritz Von Erich, and the brother of Kerry and the late David Von Erich, all of whom have had successful wrestling careers.

All three brothers, at one time or another, had been real threats to Ric Flair and his NWA world heavyweight title. Kerry got it but lost it, and Kevin came close. Some even say he won. But that's another story.

In Dallas Kevin pinned Flair in the center of the ring. When the championship belt was brought into the ring and

handed to Kevin, pandemonium broke loose. As people screamed and flashes popped, Kevin walked around the ring as proud as a peacock. Unfortunately, in minutes his brief reign of glory turned to gloom. Suddenly, referee Bruno Lubich took the belt away from Kevin and handed it back to Flair.

What really happened that fateful evening was ironic. At the beginning of the bout Kevin dominated Flair. Then Flair mounted an impressive offensive, and Kevin was on the run. However, Von Erich possesses sensational acrobatic abilities

Kevin Von Erich has Ric Flair ropeward bound.

BARRY WINDHAM

BARRY WINDHAM'S FATHER is Black Jack Mulligan. Black Jack Mulligan, Jr., decided early on that he wanted to stand on his own, and so he fought under the name Barry Windham.

Barry Windham learned well the rugged style of his father, Black Jack Mulligan, Sr., and he certainly proved that he could make it on his own as well. In his career Barry captured both the Florida heavyweight title and the Southern heavyweight title, as well as the Florida tag team championship, with partner Mike Graham.

An unfortunate car crash forced Barry to relinquish his Southern title, but after recuperating from his accident he came back tougher than ever. He then teamed up with his father, and Black Jack Mulligan, Jr., and Sr. made an invincible team. Barry Windham learned all of his dad's tricks and combined them with his scientific ability, making him a hard man to beat. Together the Black Jacks proved to be a devastating combination, winning several tag team titles.

Barry Windham went on to wrestle in Atlanta, Georgia; Knoxville, Tennessee; and the Mid-Atlantic territory. He proved his capabilities by capturing the Southern heavyweight title from Big John Studd.

A rift between father and son forced Barry to leave the southern states and return to Florida. Says Windham of his dad, "You have to wrestle the way that's best for you. He will always be a brawler. I consider myself to be a scientific wrestler."

But perhaps a combination of the two is the best way to go, for with a little of his father's aggressiveness Barry regained the Southern heavyweight title after he returned to the Sunshine State and thus found himself at war with J. J. Dillon and his stable, having some particulary harsh skirmishes with Angelo Mosca, Sr. Windham also became involved in a war

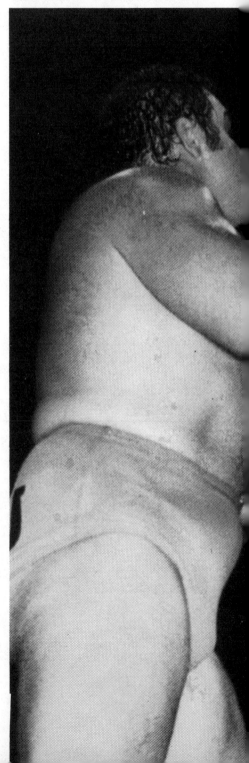

Above: Barry Windham applies his headlock to the likes of Harley Race. Right: Windham boots Ron Bass.

with the satanical Kevin Sullivan. It seemed everywhere that Windham went, chaos was sure to follow.

And then Black Jack Mulligan, Sr., arrived on the scene again, and things began to pick up for the young Barry Windham. Together with good friend Dusty Rhodes, Barry Windham and Black Jack Mulligan, Sr., formed a pack to rid Florida of all the useless scum—slime like Mosca, Sr.; Sullivan; and the Purple Haze. "Believe me," says Windham, "we will do it."

He is one determined young wrestler. At 6 feet 2 inches and 240 pounds, this hunk is well on his way to becoming one of the all-time greats of the sport.

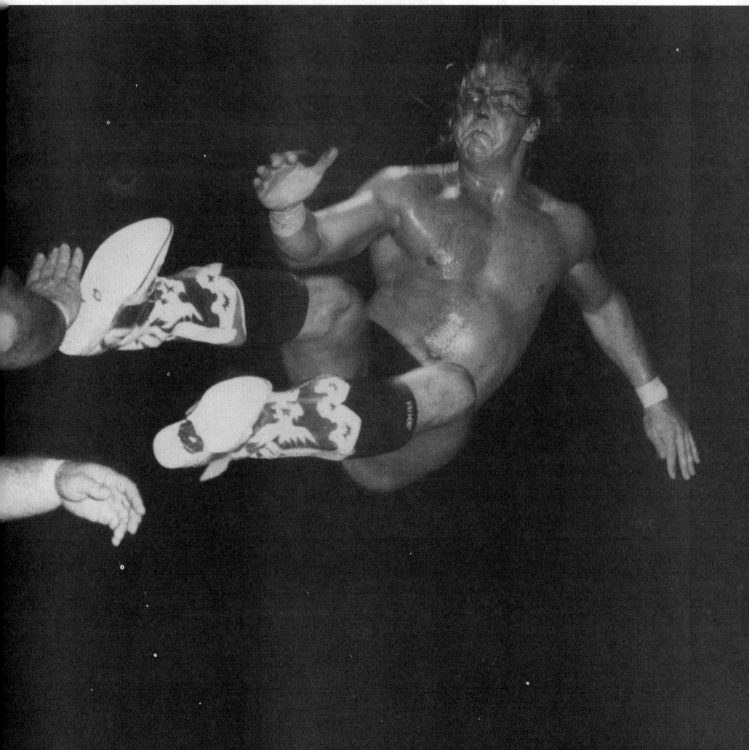

THE BAD

ADRIAN ADONIS

THE ONE THING THAT SETS Adrian Adonis apart from other so-called villains is the fact that he can wrestle. Unlike many of his evil colleagues, Adonis can execute many skillful holds and maneuvers. Of course, when the going gets tough, the tough get going, and nobody is tougher than Adrian, who can reach deep down into his bag of tricks and come up with a well-placed kick or fist to the head that will really send his opponent flying. His ability to combine scientific moves with roughhouse tactics has enabled the New York City brawler to score many impressive wins over the top stars in his sport.

When Adrian Adonis steps into the ring, the crowd is driven into a frenzy. Completely garbed in leather, the man most fans love to hate claims that he is not trying to imitate a biker, a gangster, a

roughneck, or a poof. "I just like leather," the up-front Adonis states. "It's fashionable, it's expensive, and I look good in it. But, no matter how good leather looks, I'll look even better wearing the championship belt!"

In May 1984, wrestling in the WWF, Adonis added the finishing touches to his outfit when, along with Texan Dick Murdoch, he captured the WWF tag team belt. But Adonis still looks forward to the day when he will be wearing the WWF heavyweight belt. "That's the one I

really want," proclaimed Adonis. "And what I want . . . I *always* get."

Adonis doesn't want to brag, but he will, and offers his opinion that, in his humble way, he is the best thing going in the wrestling world today. He has his eye on every championship he can see, and feels confident that there is no one better to unify the title picture. The brash and cocky leather man from New York has worked his way slowly to the top, and plans to climb even higher.

Opposite: East is east and west is west—and Adrian Adonis meets Fujinami with a best-of-all worlds flying drop kick. Right: The leather legend, Adrian Adonis, with his manager, Fred Blassie.

RON BASS

YESTERDAY A HERO, THE RON Bass of today is a hated villain. What brought about this change in the King of the Cowboys? Well, it started when Bass was asked to referee the world title bout between newly crowned champion Harley Race and two-time champion Dusty Rhodes.

The match took place a week after Harley Race regained the title for the seventh time. Having arrived in Florida, Race immediately signed to fight the American Dream, Rhodes. This angered the volatile Bass, who thought that the match should have been his.

Bass and the Dream had been friends for years. In fact, it had been Dusty who originally had asked Bass to come to Florida to help him fend off the Texas Outlaws and others who were threatening to take over the Sunshine State. Bass consequently did so well in the South

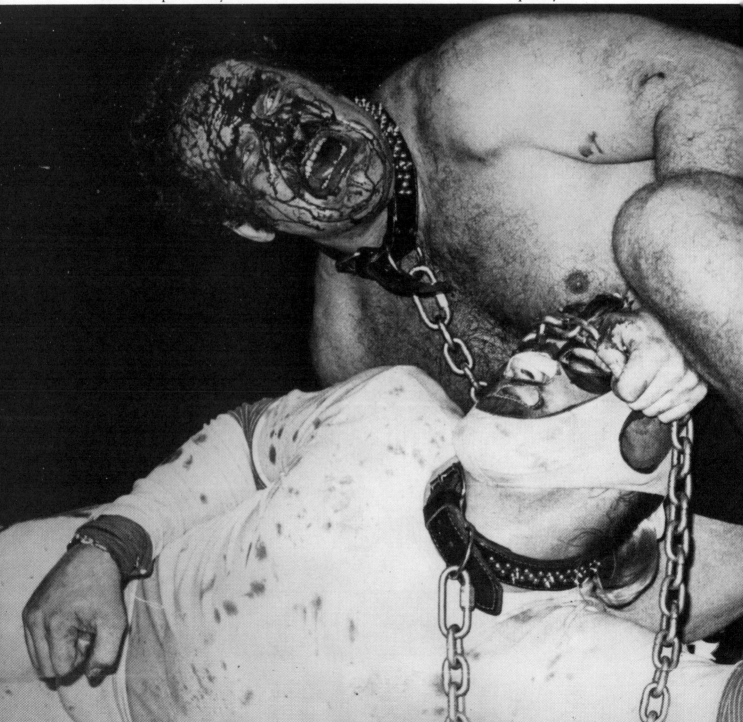

that he captured the Global tag team title with Barry Windham, as well as the prestigious Southern heavyweight belt.

The Southern title is the most respected title in Florida, and as champion Bass had effectively become the number-one wrestler in Florida. And that is why

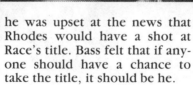

he was upset at the news that Rhodes would have a shot at Race's title. Bass felt that if anyone should have a chance to take the title, it should be he.

"I deserve that match," claimed Bass. "I earned the right to face Harley Race, and I just don't understand why I'm being passed over for Dusty Rhodes."

When Bass was asked to referee the match, he accepted. He did an excellent job of refereeing for about 45 minutes while the two wrestled, but when Dusty began to stage an offensive, the anger came out, and Bass jumped his long-time friend, mauling and beating Dusty senseless, of course ruining his own chance at the title.

After his attack on Dusty, Bass became a wanted man. Former friends were now out for blood, but somehow through it all Bass managed to retain his Southern belt.

Bass now is the most despised man in the sport, but the Cowboy has not acted alone. In his corner all along has been the despicable J. J. Dillon. Since coming under Dillon's tutelage, Bass has continued his winning ways and picked up a few new tricks as well. With the evil Dillon at his side, he is invincible.

Ron Bass sees red in his chain match with Yellow Dog.

95

JACK AND JERRY BRISCO

THIS DIABOLICAL DUO HAS undergone a transition not unlike that of Dr. Jekyll into Mr. Hyde. Once cheered and respected by everyone, Jack and Jerry Brisco are now two of the most despised individuals in the wrestling world. Every day they seem to become even more vicious than the day before. They bite, they kick, they punch, they pinch—in short, they use every illegal trick in the book.

"Look," snarls Jerry, "I'm tired of people asking us why we've changed. Winning is the bottom line, and the Briscos are on top. That ought to tell you something."

Jerry, a former NWA junior heavyweight champion, and Jack, a former NWA world heavyweight champion, know all about winning. And after watching the Briscos in action, it is quite obvious that they are one of the finest tag team combinations in the sport.

Jack Brisco is a natural wrestler. He got involved in the sport at the request of a high-school football coach who wanted to keep his players in shape between seasons. Wrestling came easy to Jack, and after a very successful amateur career, he turned pro. Although he is small for a professional, his basic wrestling skill, along with his willingness to fight fire with fire, has made him a winner.

The Briscos' battles with Ricky Steamboat and Jay Youngblood contributed greatly to their reputations as bad guys. In one of their matches Youngblood delivered a tomahawk chop to Jack. Jack fell hard, landing right on Steamboat's leg. Steamboat was in such pain that the bout was called. The fans blamed the Briscos for purposely injuring Steamboat and never forgave their favorite tag team. From then on the Briscos

were despised and jeered.

The Briscos make frequent use of the tag in their bouts, as well as employing many scientific holds. These constant tags tend to tire and wear down their opponents. Then Jack and Jerry move in for the kill with a figure four, an airplane spin, or the sleeper. These maneuvers—along with a few illegal moves the brothers have incorporated into their repertoire—have made them one of the top tag teams in the country.

But that is not enough for these two. "We want to be recognized as the best tag team in the world," says Jerry. "We have won numerous titles all over the country, but our goal is to win every major tag team championship in the world. After that we will defend our belts in Japan, Hong Kong, Australia, and anywhere else we find opposition," promises Jerry. "We are simply the greatest tag team in the sport."

Page 96: Jerry Brisco with headlock on Dory Funk.
Above: Jack Brisco has Terry Funk in an airplane spin.

KILLER BROOKS

FOR THE PAST TEN YEARS Killer Brooks has been one of the most controversial figures in wrestling. He has been an instigator in more battles and brawls than any other roughneck in the sport—and the Killer loves it. "I'm vicious," Killer admits proudly. "That's the way I was raised, and that's the way I like it. I've got a mean streak that runs from the back of my neck to the tip of my toes and don't dare cross me if you know what's good for you."

"I'm the only Killer in this sport," Brooks bellows. "And why do you think they call me Killer? Because I'm nice, friendly, happy-go-lucky? I'll tell you why, fool, if you don't know by now. My aim is to hospitalize as many people as I can, and if I'm really lucky, they won't ever make it out of their hospital beds. If anybody wants something done the right way, they call on the only man that can pull it off."

After his arrival in World Championship Wrestling territory, Killer Brooks was true to his reputation. In his first match in the Omni Brooks wrestled Paul Orndorff for the National heavyweight title. Prior to the battle, Larry Zbyszko offered Brooks $25,000 if he could defeat Orndorff and present Zbyszko with the belt. Killer, true to form, made an easy $25,000, and Zbyszko had his belt. Says Killer of the skirmish, "It was a snap. The only problem is I didn't clobber Orndorff hard enough with the chair. But my next job I know I'll do it right."

After Brooks won the belt for Zbyszko, he became Zbyszko's ally. Whenever Zbyszko needed something done, he would turn to Brooks, and so far Killer has never let him down. "I've been around a lot of top men in

my illustrious career," bragged Zbyszko, "but I've never run across anyone like Killer Brooks. He's tough, good, big, and strong, and if he makes a promise, he sticks by it."

Before he became a "rassler," Brooks collected bounties all over the West. "Once I get my sights on someone, he never escapes. Like a bloodhound, I go after my prey, and I don't let up until I have him cornered."

In Texas, his home state, and

Killer Brooks takes a moment off from mayhem to pose with his belt and battle gear.

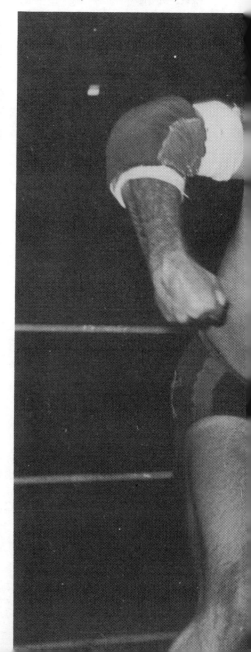

The Killer captures the rapt attention of Manny Fernandez, with a little prodding.

all over the West his accomplishments are legendary. The Killer holds victories over many big stars, including the three Von Erichs, Jose Lothario, Chavo Guerrero, and Alberto Madril. Yet he has never received the recognition he truly deserves. But this does not faze the Killer. "Look, the only thing that matters is how much green you put in your jeans. Everything else is secondary. If you make some cash, crack some heads, drink some beers, and have a hell of a good time while you're at it, that's all that matters. Titles are good, but money is better. Breaking bones and collecting bounties is my claim to fame, and that's how I'll be remembered. There's only one true Killer, and don't you forget it."

That about sums up Killer Brooks's philosophy of wrestling and his life. Although he will never be considered a standout wrestler from a technical point of view, he never fails to get the job done. At times Brooks may even use some actual wrestling holds and maneuvers, but that isn't really his style.

Total annihilation is his style, and using his own personal brand of chaos, the tough Texan has made wrestling history by breaking bones, cracking heads, and collecting large bounties all over the wrestling world.

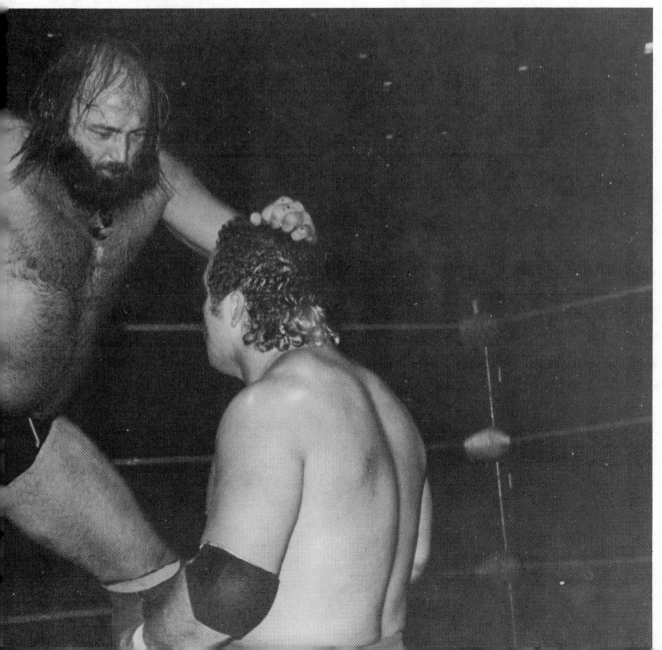

TED DiBIASE

TED DiBIASE IS A RIDDLE wrapped inside an enigma. To some he appears to be a bad, evil man; but there are others who maintain that he is, in fact, a very decent person.

Once upon a time, as all such tales start out, DiBiase was a beacon of wrestling integrity, lighting the way for all to see. Then, suddenly and without warning, he became a notorious rule breaker. The fans, who once loved him and respected him, have turned against him. And DiBiase now seems to want only to rub their noses in their own hatred—and his foes' faces in the ring mat.

Likewise, those who opposed DiBiase in the ring have come to despise him, loathe him, hate him. They believe he has turned into a savage animal—or even worse. Tommy Rich says that he is "more dangerous than an animal because an animal only demands victory at any cost, but Ted wants to inflict heinous and terrible punishment."

Something seems to be fundamentally wrong with DiBiase. Against Bob Armstrong he went berserk, literally mutilating him, breaking his cheekbones and almost destroying him. What he did to Armstrong had nothing to do with the sport of wrestling. Sure, he won the belt, but the consensus is that he won it unfairly. Much like Dracula, DiBiase has come to revel in his cruelty. "Fresh opponents," he chants, "fresh victims, fresh meat. The national title is the bait I use to trap my victims. . . ."

When pushed, DiBiase will admit that sometime in the long, long ago he loved wrestling. Now all he seems to care about is earning more and more money, more than anyone else. He sees wrestling as a job and the ring as his castle—around which he has constructed a moat. And woe to anyone who tries to enter his castle without knocking: he will be dealt with in a "Trespassers will be Prosecuted" manner, his bones broken, his head smashed, and his career ruined. It doesn't seem to faze DiBiase in the slightest that he plans to translate all those broken bones and dreams into a fortune.

DiBiase openly states that "honor is a word for jerks," and that all that matters to him is winning—at whatever cost his opponent has to pay for DiBiase's growing wealth. And reputation for exhibiting the worst wrestling can offer.

DiBiase elbows the Mysterious Mr. R. in a Baltimore bout.

Ted DiBiase puts the slug on Pat Patterson.

RIC FLAIR

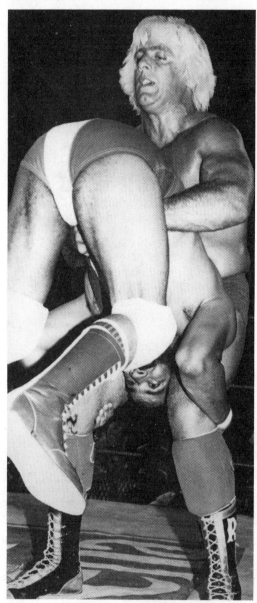

THE RIC FLAIR LEGEND BEGAN in 1972 in Minnesota, where Flair spent many grueling moments learning the ropes from Verne Gagne and Billy Robinson. But even then he knew that one day he would become a world champion.

From an early age Flair stuck with his ambition of becoming a wrestler, never losing sight of his goal. Finally, his hard work paid off. On September 17, 1981, the Nature Boy defeated Dusty Rhodes in Kansas City and became NWA world champion. It was a dream come true. But, like most dreams, it had to end, and did, two years later, when his reign as champion was terminated by Harley Race.

For the next ten months Flair's mind was set on one thing: regaining what he affectionately referred to as his "ten pounds of gold"—his belt. But try as he might, Flair could not regain his title and belt from Race, the crafty seven-time world champion, and even considered retiring from the sport, convinced he might never again regain what he viewed as rightfully his.

Finally, like the Little Train That Could, Flair made up his mind to beat Race, and he did, on the night of November 24, 1983. He regained the NWA world heavyweight championship and, just as importantly, his "ten pounds of gold." Fittingly enough, Flair's triumph came in the main event of one of wrestling's greatest extravaganzas, "Starcade '83," a super night of wrestling in Greensboro, North Carolina—an evening that saw 12 matches on the Flair-Race card. The rules for the historic confrontation between Flair and his nemesis were simple: there would be no stopping for blood, there would be no time limit, and there must be a definite winner. Over twenty thousand fans jammed the Greensboro Coliseum to watch Harley Race take a beating he would never forget. And, at the end of a particularly vicious war, Flair emerged victorious, champion once again, just as he knew he would. Flair's second reign as champion came to an end, however, on May 6, 1984, when he was defeated by Kerry Von Erich in Texas Stadium. But Flair was persistent and chased the champion to Japan. On May 24, in Tokyo, Flair defeated Von Erich to regain the world title.

Before attaining world championship status, Ric spent several years competing in the Mid-Atlantic area, developing his skills. "The Mid-Atlantic territory was a great testing ground for me," remembers Flair. "While there I faced virtually every big man in the sport and did very well against them. I captured the Mid-Atlantic title, the US title, the Mid-Atlantic tag team title, and the world tag team title. I must also say that the competition was first rate, with men like Ricky Steamboat, Greg Valentine, Jimmy 'Superfly' Snuka, Ken Patera, and Wahoo McDaniel all wrestling in the region."

Asked who was the toughest competitor he faced while active in the Mid-Atlantic area, Flair answered, "Of all the men I faced early in my career, I have to give the nod to Ricky Steamboat as my toughest competitor." But Flair progressed beyond Steamboat—far beyond him—as he went on to championship status and left his onetime adversary behind.

Ric's schedule has to be the most demanding of any champion ever to wear the world crown. He defends his title night after night, all over the globe. In one week the champion has been known to put his title on the line in Charlotte, North Carolina, on Sunday afternoon; Toronto, Canada, on Sunday evening; and then depart for a tour of the Pacific to wrestle in New Zealand, Australia, Malaysia, and the Philippines.

Although there are several other title claimants throughout the wrestling world, Ric Flair has certainly proven himself the "champion of champions." And the colorful, talented Flair promises to try to hold on to the prestigious NWA title for a long, long time.

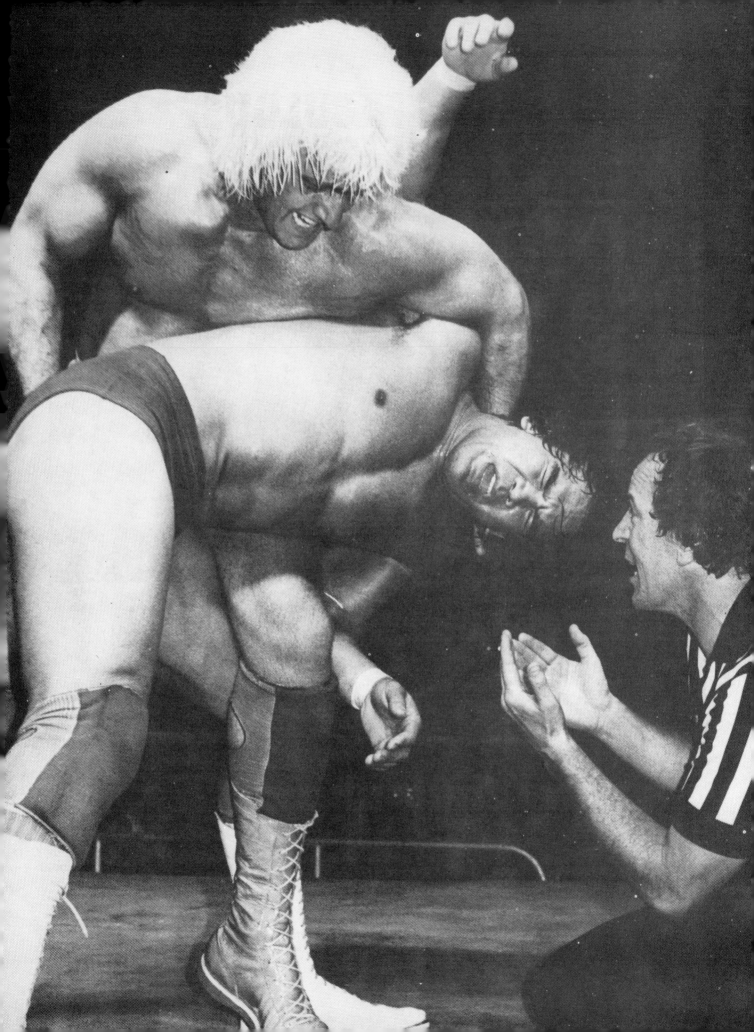

THE FABULOUS FREEBIRDS

Above: A "tri-namite" trio: Terry Gordy, Michael Hayes, and Buddy Roberts. Opposite: Hayes puts Don Kernodle to sleep with a Freebird hold.

THE FABULOUS FREEBIRDS—Michael Hayes, Terry Gordy, and Buddy Roberts—are what tag team wrestling is all about. This fearsome threesome from "Badstreet USA" have been together their entire life, and watching them in action, it shows.

"We grew up on Badstreet," boasts Hayes. "It was a street so mean that the farther you walked down, the meaner it got. And me and my brothers lived in the last house on the block! That can tell you how tough we are."

In their wrestling careers the Freebirds have held the National tag team title, the Georgia tag team championship, and the World Class Six-Man tag team championship. "Everywhere we've been we've been the best," stated Terry Gordy. "And there ain't anybody tougher in this business than me and my brothers. Understand, if there is anyone who wants to start some static just tell them to look us up because we ain't never backed down from anyone, and we ain't about to start now."

The Freebirds are unique in that all three members of the team can wrestle. This gives them a distinct advantage over their opponents, who just never know which two members of the team they will be facing. Invariably, all three Freebirds become involved in their altercations. "It doesn't matter which one of us is left on the outside," states Buddy Roberts, "because no matter who's in the ring, we work as a unit. There is no jealousy, no arguments, and no petty nonsense going on in our organization."

Besides their wrestling prowess, the Freebirds have made quite a name for themselves in rock circles. Their song, "Badstreet USA," was a big hit in Dallas and in several southern states. Michael Hayes and company are hopeful that they will land a major distribution deal. If so, look for the Freebirds to make an appearance on MTV.

The Fabulous Freebirds, with their unique style and approach, have completely revitalized the tag team scene. Expect to see the Fabulous Freebirds on or near the top of the tag team world for a long time.

"Gorgeous" Jimmy Garvin shows Chris Adams the way—across the ring with a long-distance toss.

HE MAY BE CONTROVERSIAL, but "Gorgeous" Jimmy Garvin is one of the sport's most outstanding figures and wrestlers.

Originally hailing from Florida, Garvin moved bag and baggage to Texas to seek his fortune. Prospecting around, Garvin found his future looked good in the Lone Star State, and even changed his style and attitude to match his new outlook. Soon he had hired a valet and begun to call himself Gorgeous.

Some of the Gorgeous One's detractors assert that he deliberately hides behind his valet when the going gets tough. But Garvin claims this is mere propaganda, and that his opponents are jealous of him. He says the only time he ever stepped behind his valet came when he wanted to use the act as a psychological gambit—which is in keeping with Garvin's strategy to keep his rivals guessing what his next move will be.

He also takes issue with those who claim he is a rule breaker, holding that his tactics are just wrestling's answer to one-upmanship. He is "not a rule breaker, only more aggressive" than he was in the past, an attitude he resorted to when he saw many people with less talent than he had getting ahead quicker. Forced "to rectify" the situation a little, he made up ground on the outside with imagination and attention-getting ploys. Now he stands on the threshold of greatness.

Striving for the recognition he believes he deserves, the Gorgeous One has now set his sights on becoming number one. Valet or no.

"GORGEOUS" JIMMY GARVIN

Garvin with a headlock on Adams in a San Antonio cage match.

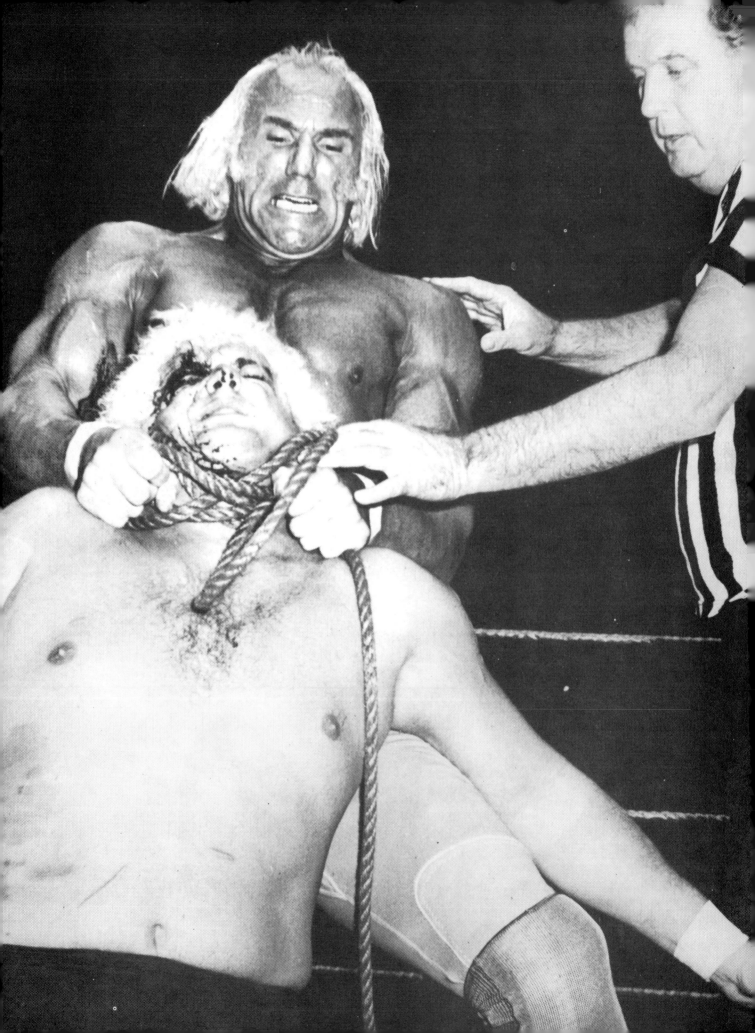

"SUPERSTAR" BILLY GRAHAM

WRESTLING MAY BE THE ONE sport in which the fan can both hate and respect a participant at the same time. If so, then "Superstar" Billy Graham is the number-one example of the fans' schizophrenia.

With an ego and arrogance that could fill a book, over the years Graham has been one of the worst offenders of rule breaking, terrorizing his opponents with his monstrous muscles and martial arts mayhem. And yet, many fans respect the ends, if not the means, of Graham's success.

Victories over Ivan Putski, Dusty Rhodes, and "Gorilla" Monsoon, among other greats and near-greats, as well as gaining the WWF title from none other than the seemingly invincible Bruno Sammartino, have given Graham unprecedented success. Yet, the Superstar's ring wars have had their peaks and valleys, and his style of combat has also experienced some dramatic changes.

When Graham took the crown from Bruno in 1977, he was a hunk of muscle without equal. Fans and foes alike may remember his "Best Arms" victory in the 1976 Pro Mr. America competition; and his power was in evidence when then-newcomer Bob Backlund took the title in 1978. Following his defeat, Superstar didn't return to the WWF until 1983 as an "all-new" Billy Graham. This time the Superstar came with less muscle and less hair, but retained all the savagery, speed, and power of the old model. In Graham's absence there had been many rumors about his physical condition—all of which soon proved to be just that, rumors. For Graham had spent his time out of the WWF mastering the martial arts of Japan.

But to know him is to loathe

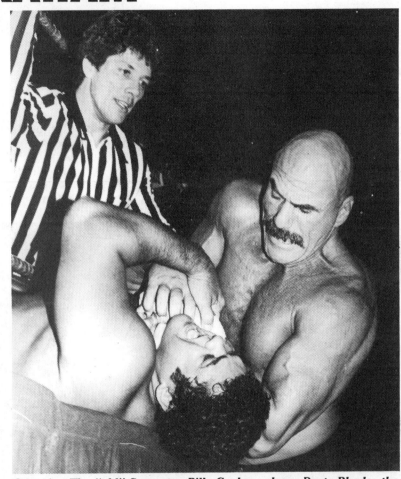

Opposite: The "old" Superstar Billy Graham shows Dusty Rhodes the ropes. Above: The "new" Superstar chokes up Pedro Morales.

him, and the old Billy we had all come to know and hate was still a big part of this martial master. And to make sure there was no mistake about just what he stood for, or stood on, he decided to mark his return by attacking Bob Backlund and ripping the title belt to shreds.

Thus, 1983 saw Backlund and Graham at war once again, and the Superstar's martial training proved every bit as tough as his muscle training had been. Still, Billy was unable to take the title, and after a few months in the WWF he began to suffer from ring burnout. "After being away for four years I just wasn't used to the traveling involved with the WWF, and my training, martial arts practice, and the rest began to suffer."

Never one to perform below the high level of expectations he sets for himself, the Superstar made the move to the AWA and then to Florida, where he captured the Florida heavyweight title.

Graham has been a major force for many years, and truly qualifies to be called Superstar. And while fans may support his quest for the title and his dedication and many talents, no one can condone his vicious acts, which seem to be the one constant in the career of "Superstar" Billy Graham.

STAN HANSEN

STAN HANSEN COMES FROM Borger, Texas. But his arena is the world, and he considers himself the uncrowned champion of the universe.

Hansen first came to national prominence in 1976, when he was hired by Fred Blassie to serve as his personal body guard—and Blassie may well have need for one, or two. Ever since then this big, bad Texan has won more titles than there are towns in his native state, recently winning the International heavyweight belt in Memphis.

Stan sincerely believes he is the best. He backs up his claim by pointing to those several titles to his credit. But he has not won the more coveted and more prestigious titles, despite some heavy prospecting. Nevertheless, Stan feels this is insignificant, because, as he puts it, "I am the highest paid wrestler in the sport today!" He believes this is so because he is a winner, and people will pay to see a winner. Anyway, he argues, he is too busy flying around the world to worry about one title in one small locale; the world is his locale, especially the Orient, where he has become a phenomenal success.

When it comes to promoting themselves, few wrestlers today can match the blustery Hansen, who seems to have cornered the market on boast and bluff. But

Stan Hansen does something wonderful to "Mr. Wonderful," Paul Orndorff.

there is a method to his egotistical madness, as he uses his braggadocio to rile up many of his opponents, much as Muhammad Ali did, bringing him many a victory when his incensed opponent loses his reason and tries to make Hansen eat his words.

For Hansen, wrestling may well be an outlet for his baser instincts. Often mean, cruel, and vicious, Hansen is reputed to be the biggest bounty hunter in the sport, and it has made him a rich man in the process—he collected $10,000 each on Dominic DeNucci, Tony Parisi, Ivan Putski, Louis Cerdan, and Bruno Sammartino. He is still looking for more.

At one time Hansen was a solo act. But he has since teamed with Bruiser Brody to form a tag team that is tough and fearsome. In the World Tag Team League tournament in Tokyo the two had a sensational victory over "Jumbo" Tsuruta and Tenryu, and were ten million yen richer as a result. He also has formed a dynamic duo with Ole Anderson, creating a team of two of the most hated grapplers in wrestling.

Stan Hansen continues on his way—deeply hated and continually winning. Both needs seem to be equal parts of the man of whom it was once said, "To know him is to loathe him."

Hansen knocks Ivan Putski hands down with an elbow.

ERNIE LADD

HE STANDS 6 FEET 9 INCHES and weighs 315 pounds. He claims to be the true "King of Wrestling." This self-proclaimed King has been on top of the wrestling world ever since he abandoned his successful football career to try his hand on the mat. He's never regretted his decision. "I demand top salary everywhere I go. My name on a card assures a sellout crowd. It's a good thing I decided to become a 'rassler,' because I am the true savior of the sport."

Ladd has been involved in a steamy feud with Andre the Giant for a long time now. "I'm literally sick and tired of that overgrown french fry and his dirty tricks. Last time I 'rassled' him I had him beat, humbled, humiliated in the center of the ring. Then, that so-called special guest referee goes and interferes on the french fry's behalf. Is that fair? I ask you.

"As far as the Giant is concerned, he's only a circus freak who's out trying to impersonate a professional heavyweight wrestler like myself. I have dignity, class, style, brains, and stamina—not to mention good looks and a great personality. The Giant ain't got any of those things. There's no way you can compare that french fry to the great Ernie Ladd. He's my main target right now . . . and as soon as I get him in that square circle I'm gonna rid the country and the wrestling world of that impostor, once and for all."

One of the King's toughest opponents was the great Bruno Sammartino. In his quest for Sammartino's title Ladd went to the trouble of hiring the services of one of the most notorious managers in the whole of wrestling, Freddie Blassie.

"That Sammartino was scared of me," boasts Ladd. "He knew that the 'Big Cat' could do him in. I first 'rassled' that Italian grape-stomper when I was just a rookie. But he never forgot the beating I laid on him that night. The old Garden was packed to the rafters with the people cheering for the Big Cat. I was clawing and chomping away at the grape-stomper so bad that the referee felt sorry for the big dude and disqualified me. If that referee hadn't stopped me, I'd have had that WWF championship. But such is life, even if I am the true king of 'rassling'."

Lately, Ernie Ladd has been trying to regain the Mid South heavyweight title. The King would love to annex this title one more time. "Look, I've held the North American belt more times than any other 'rassler,' and I'm gonna win it again and retire the title."

Love him or hate him—and most people suffer the latter emotion—Ernie Ladd calls himself the King. Perhaps someday he may even win the crown to go with his self-proclaimed kingdom.

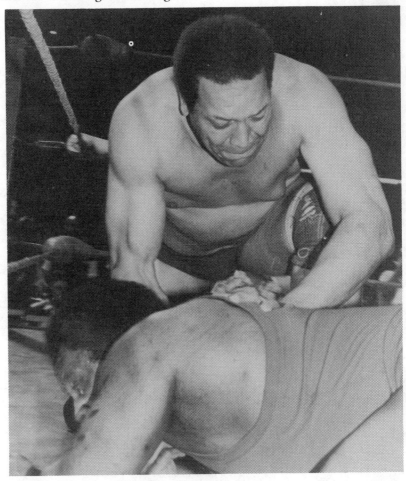

Opposite: Ernie Ladd blocks out Carlos Colon's windpipe. Above: The "Big Cat" catches Colon in his own mousetrap.

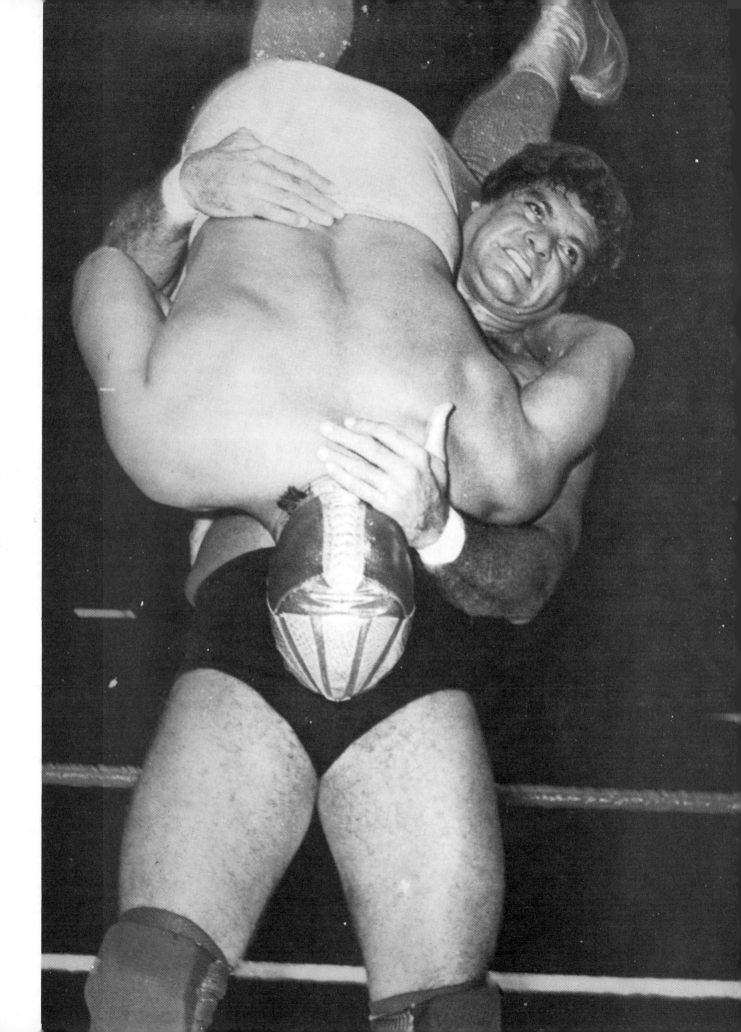

THE MAGNIFICIENT MURACO

THIS FRUSTRATED AMAZON IS fueled by anger. He speaks one moment in a calm, subdued manner, only to burst into a fit of screaming rage moments later. He seems to have some definite emotional problems, although his former manager, "Captain" Lou Albano, denies this. In the ring he will play by the rules until suddenly, without warning, he will disregard the rules and turn into a savage beast, assaulting his opponent with vicious, brutal biting and clawing.

The Captain originally brought the Magnificent Muraco into the WWF area to destroy Jimmy "Superfly" Snuka some years ago. Albano put Muraco through almost a year of intensive training before he actually put him up against Snuka. He started Muraco off with a series of bouts against Pedro Morales—bloody, nauseous affairs that might have broken the spirit of someone lesser than Muraco. Instead, they merely fed his lust for blood, and he eventually emerged victorious.

Next came several bouts against Bob Backlund. Although the Magnificent Muraco slaughtered Backlund several times, he never captured the WWF title. Frustration was building, but he would take it out on his next opponent.

The Soulman, Rocky Johnson, was Muraco's next victim. In a televised match it looked as if Johnson had beaten the Magnificent One. But it was not to be. Albano had jumped on the apron of the ring, and the referee had disqualified Muraco. Many believed this incident to be a part of Albano's master plan. Whatever the case, it led to many vicious battles with the Soulman in Madison Square Garden. When the blood ceased and the dust settled, the Magnificent One still owned the

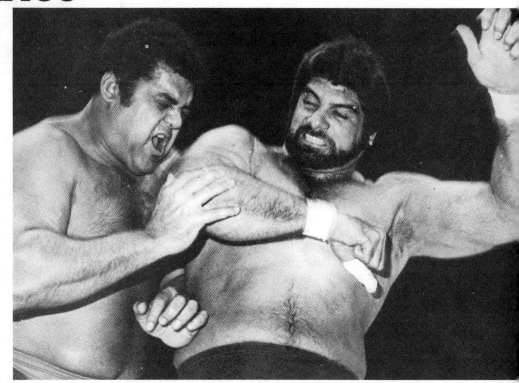

belt and all the victories.

Nearly a year after he began his training bouts Muraco was ready to face Jimmy Snuka. After Muraco insulted the hotheaded Snuka on numerous occasions, the scene was set. The first match put cockfights to shame: the bout was finally stopped when several other wrestlers had to jump into the ring to tear the two animals apart before they destroyed each other. The next battle was the same, and the referee finally disqualified both men.

Subsequent bouts ended in the same manner, and the Muraco-Snuka war has yet to be resolved.

The Magnificent One is on the road daily, facing any and all opponents, while his feud with Snuka is still brewing. But how long can this human pressure cooker keep his cool before he explodes? Someone is bound to suffer when his lid finally blows.

Opposite: Muraco carries a heavy burden—in the form of Mil Mascaras. Above: Pedro Morales tries to elbow his way through a bearded Muraco.

THE MASKED SUPERSTAR

THIS MASKED MAN'S DETERmination seems unshakable. He is on the warpath and going for for the gold—the world heavyweight championship, that is.

Although we don't know too much about him, we do know that he comes from Atlanta, Georgia, and that he tips the scales at 285 ponds. He is not only tough but quite knowledgeable about wrestling. He can expertly execute an amazing assortment of wrestling holds and maneuvers; he can wrestle scientifically, but he is also capable of becoming a rugged rule breaker. He has a tremendous capacity to absorb punishment—he can take it as well as he can dish it out! Unlike such men as George "the Animal," the Masked Superstar is in total control and knows what he's doing every second that he is in the ring. He is a professional from the word *go,* and

there is no wrestler in the sport, masked or otherwise, who takes the game more seriously.

Although it's hard to tell just how long he has been wrestling, he has spent time wrestling in the Mid-Atlantic area and has been given some stiff competition by Mr. Wrestling II and Ole Anderson. When he began wrestling there, he was not a fan favorite, but he soon won their respect with his ability.

He has also wrestled in the Mid South area of Louisiana and Texas. It was there that he originally teamed up with the Super Destroyer, creating one of the most ruthless and powerful tag teams in wrestling history.

The Masked Superstar has wrestled in Canada, battling the likes of Tony Parisi, Gino Brito, and Rick Martel. His confrontations with Dino Bravo will go down in Canadian wrestling history as some of the most intense

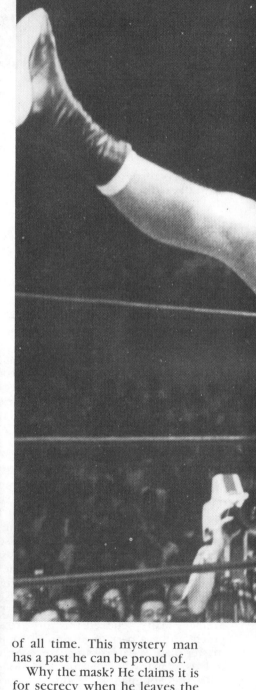

of all time. This mystery man has a past he can be proud of.

Why the mask? He claims it is for secrecy when he leaves the arena. When he takes off his mask, no one knows who he is,

and he can come and go as he pleases. Although there have been rumors that he is "Superstar" Billy Graham, he claims that he has always wrestled as the Masked Superstar.

He has said on many occasions that when he becomes the heavyweight champion he will reveal his true identity, and his one and only mission is to do just that.

Opposite: The Masked Superstar serves up Flying Fujinami. Above: The Masked Superstar and Fujinami both go airborne with an ETA imminent.

KEN PATERA

Below: Patera has Bob Backlund in a bear hug. Opposite: Patera bench presses Pat Patterson.

AMAZING FEATS OF STRENGTH have become commonplace in wrestling: Bruno Sammartino, the Road Warriors, and their many beefy counterparts would bring fear to most power-lifting champions. And let's not forget Tony Atlas, Billy Graham, and others who are as dynamically muscled as any Mr. Olympia. The question is, however, who's the strongest? The resounding answer from those in the know is Ken Patera.

Patera is a former amateur weight-lifting champion and, as such, set 28 world records. He also "snatched" the bronze medal in the 1972 Olympics as a super heavyweight for the United States and was the first American to raise 500 pounds over his head. While Ken loved the Olympic competition and spirit, it didn't compare to the flash and cash offered by professional wrestling. "Those Olympic medals may look great, but they make for a lousy meal!" says the strongman.

The transition from strongman to wrestler was an easy one for Ken, for many of wrestling's top names trained in the same gyms Patera frequented and gave him invaluable advice and experience. This experience soon was translated into Ken's infamous swinging neck breaker, a variation on the full nelson that brought Patera to the status of a top contender. Not incidentally, this move left its merciless mark on such greats as Pedro Morales, Hulk Hogan, and, most notably, Billy White Wolf, whose ride in Patera's arms landed him in the hospital.

Still, all of Ken's success has yet to earn him a major solo title belt. Few will forget his wars with champions Bob Backlund and Harley Race; but when the dust had settled, it was not Patera who left with the championship belt, it was always his adversaries. This seeming inability to land a title the equal of his massive body and even larger ego has made Ken the victim of criticism and cynicism: "He's a choker" and "He's not mentally tough enough" seem to be the most common jibes directed at Patera.

Money is what originally brought Patera into the wrestling profession. And the prospects of a large monetary gain landed him a new tag team partner, "Crusher" Jerry Blackwell. Yet, newfound wealth did not come without a heavy price. For Patera and Blackwell had to denounce the USA and become "honorary" sheiks under the guidance of Sheik Adnan el Kassey of Iraq. As Greg Gagne, capturing the thoughts of many wrestling fans, said, "Ken's totally forgotten the American ideals to which he devoted so much of his life, and now his whole philosophy has been consumed by greed."

Ken's reply was, "I know the price that has to be paid to reach the top. I know all too well the dues that have to be paid. Mine are just about paid up. The very best is yet to come for Ken Patera."

Fame and riches are now Patera's. But how far will he progress? Does the onetime all-American have what it takes to become a world champion? "I assure you that I have yet to reach my full, awesome potential," he says. The wrestling world will be eagerly awaiting Ken Patera's next plateau.

RODDY PIPER

BORN IN GLASGOW, SCOTland, and raised in Australia, Roddy Piper began wrestling at the age of six. At 16 he started his professional wrestling career in Winnepeg, Canada, and was the youngest professional wrestler ever to wrestle there. At 20 he became the lightweight champion of the world, again the youngest wrestler to achieve that distinction. He has held such titles as those of the America's championship and the America's tag team championship. He also has defeated NWA world heavyweight champion Ric Flair for the US heavyweight championship.

With a record like that, it's no wonder few wrestlers want to tangle with this lad.

Roddy is unforgettable when he enters the ring, because he wears a kilt displaying his clan's colors and plays his bagpipes. He is proud of his background, and he is proud of his wrestling skills. He has been at odds with many a wrestler, including the likes of the Magnificent Muraco, Jimmy "Superfly" Snuka, Ole Anderson, and even Andre the Giant. One of his most explosive feuds, however, has been with Greg Valentine. He and Valentine have waged war in almost every southern arena, with both Valentine and Piper suffering injuries at the hands of the other. In these wars the US heavyweight championship title changed hands several times, but the belt was only secondary in importance to the two wrestlers, whose mutual priority is the total destruction of each other.

Piper's flamboyant style and ringside mannerisms have brought him many fans and enemies alike. He is loved in the Mid-Atlantic area, booed in the Caribbean, revered in Georgia, yet despised in the WWF. But like the wind, Piper's popularity is constantly changing.

"I've always wrestled the same way," explains Roddy. "Yet in different areas, people take to me in different ways."

Roddy made a name for himself in the mid-1970's on the West Coast when he captured the prestigious America's heavyweight title. "California was a real test for me," says Roddy. "It was there that I put it all together. I held the America's title on numerous occasions besides owning the America's tag team championship and managing my own stable of champions. Once I had all these things, I thought I had it made."

But Roddy found even more challenges waiting to be met. He left California and wound up in the Pacific Northwest. But wherever he has gone, the skinny kid in the kilt has done well. He has won every major championship belt he has competed for except for the big one—the NWA world heavyweight championship held by Ric Flair, the WWF title, or the AWA crown. Roddy is quite confident, however, that he will eventually capture one if not all three of these major titles.

Roddy Piper may be a wee bit of a braggart, but he can back it up. Piper is a complete professional. He is an excellent commentator as well as a fine and experienced fighter.

Opposite: "Rowdy" Roddy Piper toots his own horn. Above: Piper gives Wahoo McDaniel a scotch treat.

Obviously, Harley Race takes his championship belt very seriously.

THE ONLY MAN TO WIN THE NWA world title on seven different occasions, Harley Race is one mean pile of muscle. Everyone's goal is to be number one, but Harley Race has held the NWA title more times than most wrestlers even get a shot at it.

The Kansas City Brawler knows what it's like to travel around the world as a wanted man. His seventh championship win, over Ric Flair, was considered a fluke by many, but Race is anxious to win the title an eighth time.

"I am back on top again, and no one is going to take the title from me," boasted Race, after capturing the title for the lucky seventh time. Although Race felt that his reign will last forever, there were many talented contenders all over the world waiting for a crack at his crown. At the top of the list applying for the potential occupancy was none other than former champion Ric Flair.

"As champion, Harley Race will be passing through the Mid-Atlantic area," stated Flair, with as much conviction as hope. "You can bet I'll be ready for him. I hope he's managed to hang onto the belt until he gets here, because I'll be waiting to take it back."

After stealing the title from Flair on June 10, 1983, in St. Louis, Race defended his crown against the likes of Dewey Robertson, two-time champ Dusty Rhodes, Florida champion Scott McGhee, and Barry Windham. Next came Stan Hansen in

Harley Race and Kerry Von Erich take a television "break."

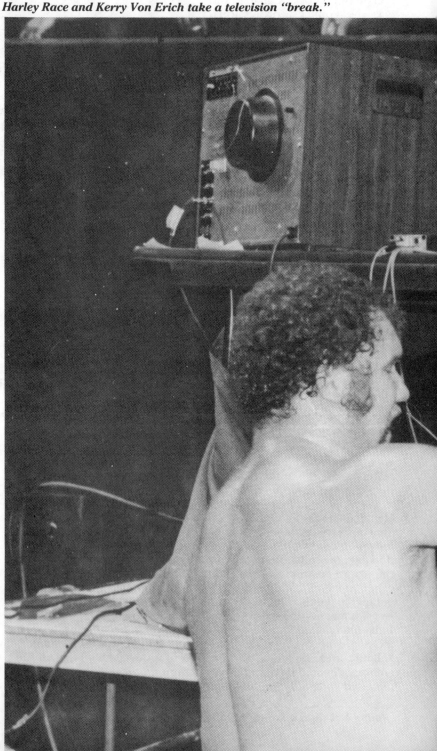

HARLEY RACE

Cleveland and then, on to Greensboro, North Carolina, to take on former champion Ric Flair in yet another return bout, this one a steel-cage match on Thanksgiving, 1983.

There were fireworks from the very first moment Race and Flair entered the arena. The flamboyant Flair made a gallant attempt to regain his belt, and finally, after a wild 25-minute brawl inside the steel cage, he did.

But don't count Harley Race out. No one yet has. With every one of his bouts a Race "riot," you can bet Harley will be back.

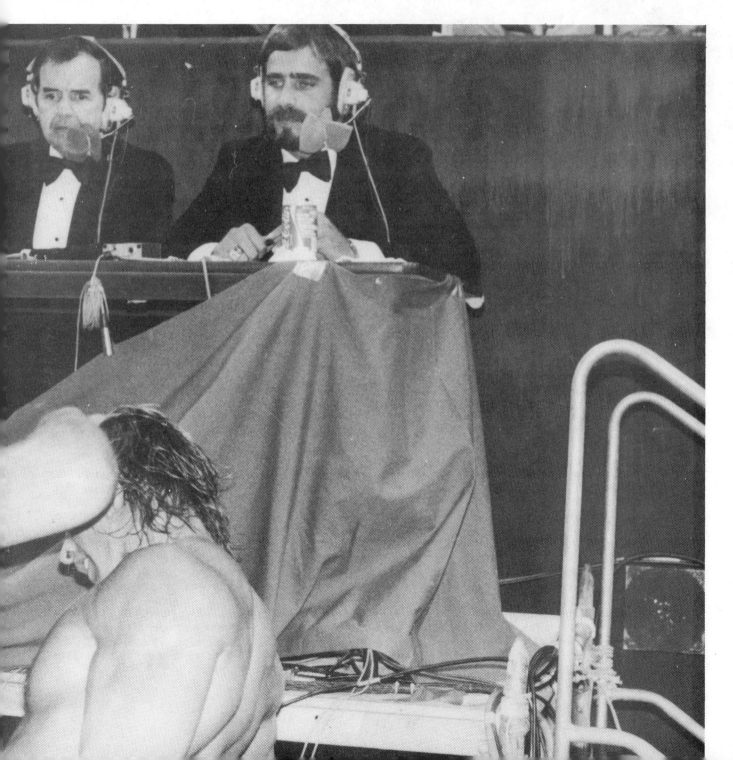

"HACKSAW" BUTCH REED

Reed and Junkyard Dog match strength to see who comes out the top dog.

"Hacksaw" Butch Reed applies the wood to the head of Junkyard Dog.

ONCE LOVED BY ONE AND all, Butch Reed has had a change of heart. In Florida and later in Georgia, Ohio, Michigan, and West Virginia, Reed was once one of the most well liked and talented wrestlers. Wrestling in Florida, Georgia, and Ohio, Reed came quite close to winning the NWA world title from champion Ric Flair.

Butch left the South and traveled to the Mid South territory and again became a fan favorite. But for some reason Reed was unable to attain the star status that he had gained in other areas. He couldn't stand to see the Junkyard Dog gathering all the fans' attention while he went by unnoticed. One day Reed could contain himself no longer and, taking matters into his own hands, launched a vicious attack on the Mid South's hero, the Junkyard Dog. After his rampage, "Hacksaw" Butch Reed got his wish: he became a hated man.

Why would he do such a thing? Reed's answer: "For recognition! The people were real-ly sick of the Junkyard Dog. They needed someone to look up to. The people knew I was better than the Dog."

Reed might have been stuck in preliminary matches before, but now Hacksaw was on top, even if it cost him the adulation of his fans.

Reed and the Dog have battled all over the Mid South area since their initial skirmish. They have each won some of the matches, and their vendetta is one of the wildest ever to hit the Mid South area. There seems to be no end in sight to this senseless brawling.

Says the Dog of Hacksaw, "I tried to be friendly with him. In fact, I was the one who brought him here to be my partner. But no, he wanted all the glory for himself.

"He thought he could get by on his past record. Well, his past record is like yesterday's newspaper. The people want to see action. They waited to see him produce, and he didn't. He couldn't stand to see guys like myself get all the support. He did what he thought he had to do, but he will have to pay for his deeds." Then the Dog said emphatically, "Hacksaw Reed, you've bitten off more than you can chew this time. The Dog is going to give you a whipping you'll never forget."

When Reed learned of Junkyard Dog's comments, he laughed. "What a joke! That man is living in a fantasy world. There's no way that he will ever be able to make me leave this area. I'm king around here now, and the Dog will never get my title."

It will be interesting to see what happens in the future. Hacksaw Butch Reed can be mean and ugly when he wants something. And what he wants is to remain king of the Mid South.

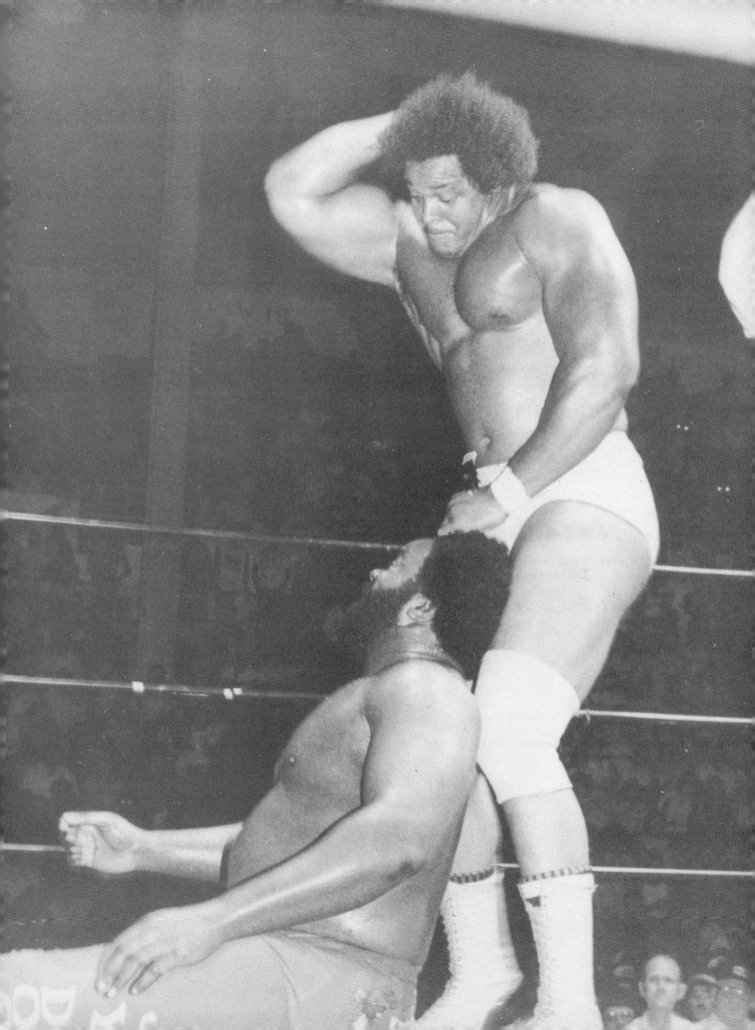

THE ROAD WARRIORS

Above: Hawk gives Jimmy Valiant a special dose of his own brand of mayhem.

Opposite: Animal and Hawk in a familiar —and family— pose.

THIS SAGA BEGINS ON CHICAgo's South Side with an infamous motorcycle gang—which now prefers to claim no part of its famous ex-members—and climaxes, less than a year later, with the National tag team belt. It is a story made up of a unique brand of wrestling that combines the disparate elements of size and strength with hideously painted faces, wild haircuts, and lots of leather. Of course, this is the story of Hawk and Animal, the awesome Road Warriors.

Other than these few physical details, little is known about these massively muscled mutants. We do know that their combined weight is over 560 pounds, that they're in their twenties, and that the purpose of their ring battles is victory, pure and simple—or impure and hard. Wrestling, by any conventional standard, has little to do with their quest for victory. "We can compete on the

theory that you throw your best shot, and we'll throw ours and see who comes out on top," stated their manager, "Precious" Paul Ellering. Using this approach they have been very successful. The great Ole Anderson has compared them to "a couple of tanks that just roll over everyone in their path."

This dynamic duo was the first team to join Ellering's army, which has included such wrestling standouts as Jake "the Snake" Roberts, the Spoiler, the Iron Sheik, and Buzz Sawyer. But when the Warriors met Sawyer, his cocky attitude earned him a broken arm, Road Warriors style. A broken arm was the least of Buzz's worries, however, as the Road Warriors have promised to maim him whenever they meet. Hawk and Animal's peculiar brand of treachery at one time also turned on the Precious One himself, when the Warriors went AWOL to go it alone. When Paul tried to remedy the situation, the Road Warriors beat him like a common street dog. As Animal snarled, "Why should we split the money three ways instead of just two?"

Expert commentator Gordon Solie voiced the feelings about the Road Warriors when he said, "I've watched a lot of men in professional wrestling over the years, but I have never seen wrestlers as completely vicious and overwhelming as these two men. Besides being tremendous athletes and incredible specimens, they have developed a bent and twisted attitude, rolling roughshod over everybody. . . ."

Today the Road Warriors are back on friendly terms with Ellering, and there just seems to be no stopping the Warriors' leather-laden street justice. These two wild ones are just bad to the bone.

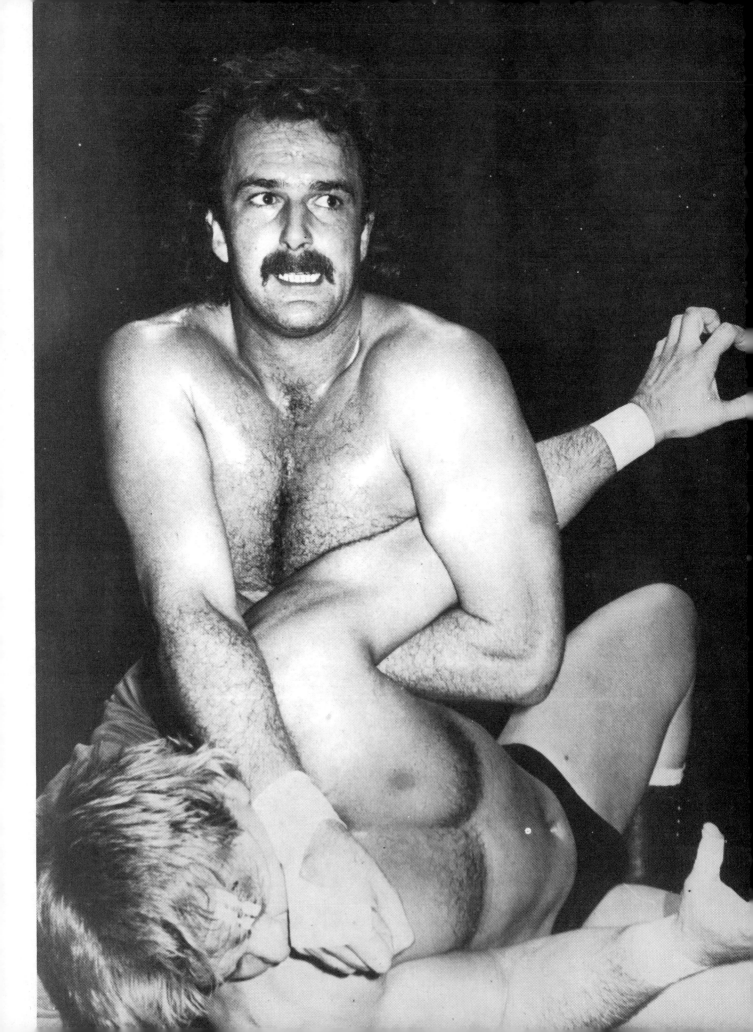

JAKE "THE SNAKE" ROBERTS

HE WAS PART OF "PRECIOUS" Paul Ellering's Legion of Doom—some would even say that he was the head man; he's been in the ring for seven hard years, and he's hated and feared by both fans and opponents. His name is Jake Roberts. But his nickname, "the Snake," seems to fit better. Jake began his wrestling career following the rules, but he soon discovered, "Something was wrong. I was losing, and needed to turn my program around. In the world of today a wrestler's got to do anything it takes for a victory."

The Snake has made steady progress, first under Keven Sullivan in Florida, then with Paul Jones in the Mid-Atlantic area, and, most recently, under Paul Ellering in Georgia for World Championship Wrestling. It was Ellering and the national TV exposure Atlantic wrestling receives that brought Jake to the forefront of present-day ring warriors. Yet, for all the exposure and contacts, the main reason for Jake "the Snake" Roberts's stature in the wrestling scene is his brutal style.

With Ellering's guidance, the Snake landed a shot at the world TV title and was soon wearing the belt. Ellering's promotion and Jake's ring terror have also led to memorable matches with Tommy Rich, Brett Wayne, and Buzz Sawyer. Few will forget the Snake's match with Wayne in which, according to Jake, "I would have had the National championship had Sawyer not added in his two cents' worth." Before that it was Ole Anderson who interfered in a grudge match between Wayne and Roberts. In true Snake fashion, Jake says, "I paid Ole back with a similar favor—I interfered in one of his matches. I took my belt off and whipped him for stepping out of line." Of course, antics like this are not

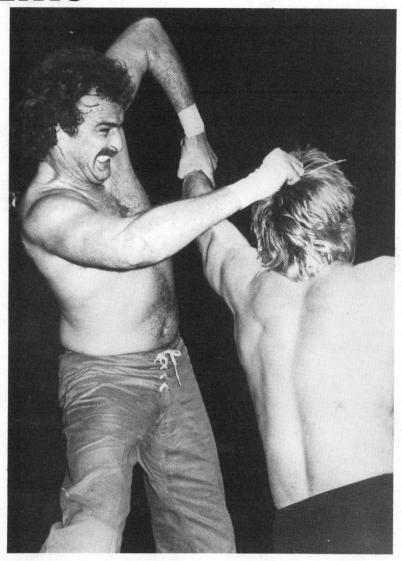

new or infrequent for Roberts. Jake says, "No one's going to get in my way. I'll do what I have to to keep people in line!"

Jake means what he says. And it's something that doesn't stop with opponents; it extends to fans, too. "I don't have time for them anymore," says Jake, who won't deal with the fans. "I realize that every time they're in my face they're taking a breath from me."

Roberts plans on "being at the top of heap" in his dealings with the Legion of Doom. And

even Paul Ellering "can be phased out if he fails to come through with good promotions and proper handling of my paperwork." So much for gratitude!

Jake's goal is the world championship, and he's been moving progressively closer to it. He is without fear and has been putting on weight and gaining skills each and every year. He says he's paid his dues and now wants the big title. "Pity the man who tries to get in my way!"

Opposite: Roberts applies his own cobralike clutch to "Gorgeous" Jimmy Garvin. Above: The Snake gets "Gorgeous" Jimmy's hair in a forelock.

"PLAYBOY" BUDDY ROSE

FOR THE PAST TWO YEARS "Playboy" Buddy Rose has been the toast of the West Coast. In fact, he's burned it up. Then, the playboy of the West Coast world wrestled on the East Coast in the WWF area and nearly captured its title. "After literally controlling the West Coast, I decided to hop in my Learjet and come east to give the women a treat. That punk Bob Backlund was afraid of me. He refused to come west. So I went east, and I crippled the punk the first chance I got. My records on the West Coast are legendary, and I was just as successful in the East, as well."

In the ring, the Playboy does display a great deal of wrestling knowledge. Observing his matches, it is obvious that he has been schooled by the best, and he exhibits many different holds and maneuvers. He is extremely agile for a big man. It is not uncommon to see Rose come charging off the ropes and deliver a flying elbow smash or a drop kick during his matches. The pet maneuvers that he often uses are his back breaker and his devastating "bombs away." When Rose's 275 pounds come flying off the top rope, it's curtains for his hapless opponent.

It is obvious, too, that the Playboy has many other things on his mind other than wasting his time in a gym lifting dumbbells. "I'm a wrestler," claims the Playboy. "I depend on my mind. I study matches, decipher them in my brain, and then spend my time relaxing in my mansion, surrounded by lots of women."

Rose very definitely portrays the image of the Playboy. He is constantly in the company of women and is quite proud of his prowess as a lady's man. "I make plenty of money, and I'm

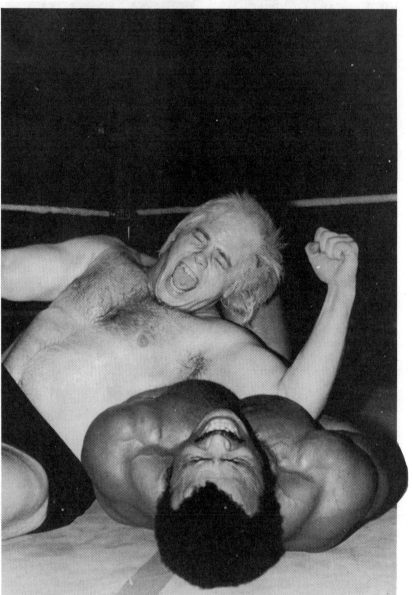

Above: "Playboy" Buddy Rose rocks Rocky "Soulman" Johnson. Opposite: Putting his best foot forward, Rose goes for a Johnson "roll."

not afraid to spend it either. I own several limousines and even a Learjet. I fly to Vegas on my days off and jet down to the casinos in the Caribbean when I feel like it. I'm on a first-name basis with the bigwigs in Monte Carlo, and I even fly to Atlantic City to rub elbows with the common folk at the roulette tables every once in a while. Women flock to me wherever I go because I show them a good time and they love it. I've been told by women that if sex were an Olympic sport, I would receive a gold medal. Eat your heart out, Tony Atlas, Tony Ga-

rea, and Bob Backlund. You wish you were like me, but there's only one me, often imitated but never duplicated!''

Buddy Rose is not ashamed about being his own best PR man. We can see that he is popular with the ladies, but can he really wrestle? ''What do you think?'' asks the infuriated Playboy. ''That I've been making up stories about my past successes? Look, I've been schooled by the best. I've trained with Verne Gagne and Billy Robinson, just as Ric Flair did, Greg Gagne, Jim Brunzell, and even Bob Backlund. This should tell you something about my background. Everyone knows his records, but for some reason no one publicizes what I've accomplished. But soon my name and reputation will be spread throughout the land when I become champion of the world!''

BUZZ SAWYER

BUZZ SAWYER IS A MAN POS-
sessed, a man who never gives
up, or lets up. In fact, he is the
perfect example of the proverbial "mad dog."

Sawyer was not always the
feared Mad Dog. At one time his
tactics and attitude were those
of a gentlemanly wrestler, one
who knew, and abided by, the
rule book. But then Sawyer, see-
ing that his good conduct may
have been winning him ribbons
but little else, changed his style.
And his tune. Now he whistles
all the way to the bank with his
bloody tactics, the scientific
ones having paid nothing.

Buzz became one of the most
hated figures ever to enter the
wrestling ring. As his actions inside the ring became more brutal and animalistic, so, too, did
his personality outside the ring.
He ceased to speak at inter-
views, instead growling like a
mad dog and snapping at everyone in sight. His attitude outside
is little different from that
within the ring, where he attacks his opponents like a rabid
dog, pounding them senseless
after they already are helpless.

Although he has always been
a mean, nasty person, there
seems to be no end to his nasti-
ness. And it grows more diabolical with each passing day. Now
he appears almost to be possessed by the devil, unfearing
and unfeeling. It's almost as if
he lives for nothing other than
to bash his opponents into
plowshares and into ring posts.
The Mad Dog hatred of all has
been inbred in him. Someone
has to tame him, even if it's just
the ASPCA.

*Sawyer models the latest style in
chains.*

Buzz Sawyer makes "the American Dream," Dusty Rhodes, have nightmares with a figure-four leglock.

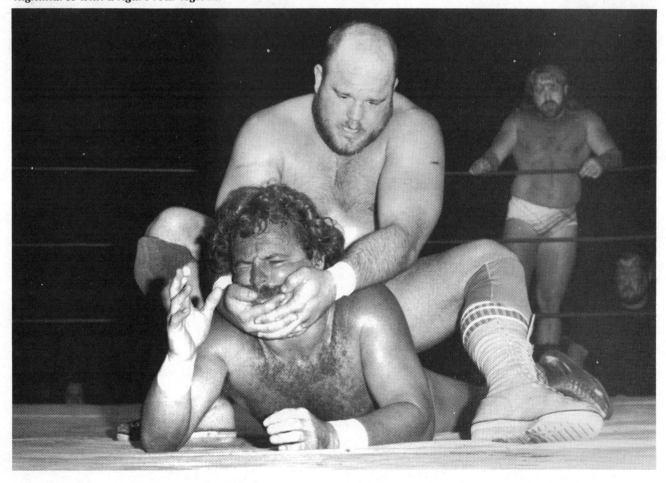

Sawyer tries a little pre-frontal lobotomy on the head of Mike Graham.

DICK SLATER

IN 1984 TAMPA, FLORIDA, NA-tive Dick Slater went to the Car-olinas and quickly carted off two championship belts. But that's not enough for the ego-centric competitor. He vows not to stop his roughneck ways until he's number one.

"I have an ego problem that constantly needs to be satis-fied," admits Slater. "When I saw that I was rated number seven in the country, I was glad, but that's not good enough. I want to be number one! I want to be known as the true king, and I don't care what it takes to get me there."

True to his word, "Dirty" Dick Slater has been racking up victory after victory. For the past nine years the baby-faced rule breaker has proven to fans, referees, and sportswriters alike that he is certainly among the most active and successful wrestlers around. He is not about to let his reputation tar-nish, either.

Says Slater, "I feel great; in fact, I've never felt better in my entire life. Right now I know that soon I will be world cham-pion." Slater works out at least four days a week, tries to get eight hours' sleep each night, and watches his diet carefully. "I'm ready and fully prepared for anything," he roars.

During 1984 Dick Slater grab-bed the Mid-Atlantic and US championship belts and was a major reason why Greg Valen-tine left the South and headed for the Big Apple.

"I don't deny that I'm rough with my opponents," he says openly. "Wrestling is a tough sport, and I see no reason not to be mean and sadistic. I'm sel-dom disqualified, so that must mean I'm not as bad as people say. I think wrestlers are just jealous when they complain to the referee that I'm cheating or breaking the rules. I think they're just afraid of me. I'm

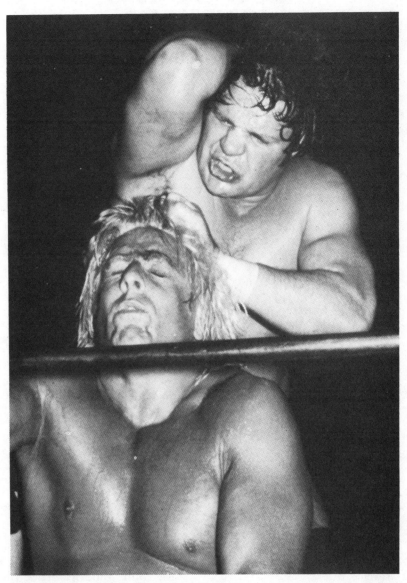

Opposite: Dick Slater flings Greg Valentine to the mat. Above: Slater resorts to cruel and unusual punishment on Ric Flair.

willing to take on anyone, but I'm running out of opponents."

Slater has had some rugged battles with topnotchers Rick Martel; Ray Stevens; Pat Patter-son; Dusty Rhodes; Dory Funk, Jr.; former NWA world cham-pion Harley Race; and current champ Ric Flair. He has more than held his own against each of them, but on occasion even this tough champion has been banged up more than he'd like to admit.

It is true that hordes of fans turn out to watch Slater wrestle.

But it is questionable whether they come to watch him win or lose. Most ringsiders would not hesitate to admit that they'd rather see him beaten. The fans complain that he kicks and bites and brings concealed weapons into the ring. They say that he wrestles like a crazy animal and that he's always breaking the rules.

But none can deny his suc-cess. Time will tell just how long it will last. One thing is for sure, however: Dick Slater has always been a winner!

BIG JOHN STUDD

"I AM THE BIGGEST, MEAN-est, baddest man in the sport!" boasts Big John Studd. At 360 pounds he definitely is the biggest professional wrestler in the sport today—with one exception, that is. Andre the Giant is still one up on Big John, and that makes the Studd mad!

"No one, and I repeat no one, can match my awesome strength and power," claims the huge brute. He also claims that people in the sport overlook him and that he is going to change all that. It is hard to imagine anyone overlooking him, however.

Studd is his own best PR man and is quick to proclaim his praises and brag about his victories over the likes of Black Jack Mulligan and Bruiser Brody. However, there is one name he is not so quick to mention, and that is Andre the Giant. Whenever his name comes up, Studd will make a remark like, "Do you mean to say that you have the audacity to put Andre the Giant in the same category as me? That man is a freak! He's not a wrestler, he's a circus sideshow. I am a legitimate wrestler. I am an athlete. I take the sport seriously. Andre the Giant is a disgrace to my profession."

Although Big John may not think so, he definitely does belong in the same category as the Giant. In fact, the Giant is one notch higher than Studd, and until Studd faces that fact—and defeats Andre in the ring—he cannot rightfully claim himself

the biggest and the baddest.

Big John Studd's former manager, Fred Blassie, says, "If Andre the Giant has the nerve to be embarrassed by Big John, let him put his X on the dotted line. After Big John takes care of him, Andre the Giant can retire to Hollywood where he belongs and make his living playing the lead in monster movies."

Aside from his preoccupation with Andre the Giant and prior to his arrival in the WWF area, Big John Studd terrorized Florida. Managed by the infamous J. J. Dillon, he posed a menacing threat to all wrestlers in the Sunshine State.

"One thing I will always remember about Florida is Dusty Rhodes," muses the egotistical Studd. "One day our paths will meet again, and Dusty will be reduced to Dust. He'll leave the arena in a ceramic urn, and his manager can sprinkle him over the ocean."

Another big name that Big John is anxious to conquer is Hulk Hogan. "He can run but he cannot hide. And when I catch him, he'll wish he could hide for the rest of his life, 'cause after I get through with him, he's not going to want to show his face anywhere."

Big John Studd has made his presence known in the wrestling world, but he still must prove himself with actions and not just the words of a braggart. If he can squash Andre the Giant, then he will truly be the biggest, the meanest, and the baddest.

Big John Studd sends Bob Backlund up, up, and away.

Kevin Sullivan has more than an armful of "the American Dream," Dusty Rhodes.

EVER SINCE KEVIN SULLIVAN came on the wrestling scene, Florida has not been the same. Only when the Satanical One is finally driven out of the sport will wrestling return to normal.

Dressed in a black cloak with a hood partially concealing his face, Sullivan makes his sinister prediction: "Right now we are in the final days. Every step is falling into place. One day soon, whether he wants it or not, Dusty Rhodes and I will wrestle side by side. Then he's mine."

The evil Sullivan's reign of terror has gripped the entire state. Sullivan's continuous assaults on Dusty Rhodes and the "Family" have left fans awestruck. They may have thought they'd seen every kind of evil that Sullivan is capable of creating, but now Sullivan is up to a new plan. First he brought in a demonic adversary, a mysterious mute wrestler who appears totally dominated by Sullivan. Then, it was Kharma, disguised as the Midnight Rider, who came to Sullivan's rescue during a controversial match between Sullivan and Dusty Rhodes in Lakeland, Florida. Rhodes had Sullivan in an excrutiating leg lock, and just when it seemed that Sullivan would be forced to submit, Kharma jumped into the ring and bludgeoned Rhodes across the back of the neck, hoisted Sullivan up across his massive shoulders, and left the ring.

Sullivan later added another evil disciple to his ranks, as if the allegiance of Kharma weren't enough—Buzz Sawyer, who, through Sullivan's hypnotic powers, underwent a total personality change. Sawyer allowed Sullivan to fasten a dog collar around his neck and lead him around the ring on all

KEVIN SULLIVAN

fours, growling and panting. "Kharma and Sawyer are extensions of me," claimed the evil Sullivan. "I am their spiritual adviser. I council them on cosmic wisdom."

What is the story behind the insatiable hatred between Sullivan and Dusty Rhodes? "Ten years ago I was here when Virgil Runnels became the star-spangled boy, the American dream, that everyone was in love with," Sullivan explains bitterly. "I was partners with Mike Graham then, and I went to all the victory parties and lived the sweet life with them. Then I had to leave for Japan, and when I came back, Mike Graham had hitched himself to the rising superstar Dusty Rhodes. I was forced to leave Florida while he enjoyed the good life. If they had asked me to stay and be part of the Family, I wouldn't be the way I am." Sullivan's eyes glisten with hate. "I am Dusty's bad karma."

Rhodes, on the other hand, wants to get revenge against Sullivan, who threw a bottle of ink in Dusty's sister's face at Dusty's tenth anniversary celebration.

Sullivan is philosophical about his situation. "Dusty Rhodes should understand by now that I hold the power, that I have the key to his very survival. I am the ying to his yang; I am the night to his day; I am the moon to his sun. Without me, Dusty Rhodes can't exist because I am the mirror image of him. When he looks at me, he sees the evil that is locked inside himself waiting to come out. He wants this as much as I want it. He wants someone to push him in the direction where he will finally make a stand and say, 'Yes, I am evil; I am darkness; I am a servant of Kevin Sullivan's.'"

The venomous Kevin Sullivan.

GREG VALENTINE

Opposite: Greg Valentine sends more than hearts and flowers Pedro Morales's way. Above: A bloody Valentine's day.

GREG "THE HAMMER" VALENtine, from Seattle, Washington, is one of the most devastating stars in the sport. He is a methodical wrestler who can do many things inside the ring. His moves are flawless, while his chops and smashes are simply deadly.

In his career Valentine has won awards all over the country. His collection of titles includes the US belt, the Mid-Atlantic championship, the America's title, and the NWF championship. Right now the Hammer is hoping to add either the WWF or the NWA title to his résumé. "Look, I've won every state and regional title in the US," Valentine bragged. "I've wrestled Flair for the NWA belt on a couple of occasions, but I always got a raw deal. The same thing happened against Hulk Hogan when I battled him for his WWF belt. But, I'm not giving up yet. I know that I am the best and I am determined to prove this fact to the world."

Greg Valentine has been managed by both the late Grand Wizard and "Captain" Lou Albano. Both have helped his career tremendously, but Valentine has a warm spot in his heart for the Wiz! "The Wiz was the greatest," Valentine states. "Even though he was never a wrestler himself, he knew so much about the sport. I owe a great deal of my success to his wisdom and guidance. I'll never forget him."

Although Greg Valentine is considered a villain, the blond bomber never resorts to out-and-out illegal moves to win his bouts. He is rough and tough and likes it that way. Valentine's attack is relentless—he simply pounds his opponents until they are tired out and worn down to the point where they are on the verge of defeat. Then he moves in for the kill using his feared flying elbow smash.

Using this technique Greg Valentine has been very successful. "If success is measured in the number of titles you win, you can say that I've been very successful," Valentine states. "But there's still more for me to accomplish."

Greg Valentine is the consummate wrestler. He's been on top for quite a number of years, and it is inevitable that there he will remain for many more.

JESSE "THE BODY" VENTURA

JESSE VENTURA PROUDLY calls himself "the Body," because he wholeheartedly believes that he has the most magnificent physique in all the world. Gloating over the fact that it is his right and privilege to call himself "the Body," Ventura will defend that right in the ring or out, underlining in the most obnoxious terms his certainty that no one anywhere has a more perfect body.

Ventura also believes he is undefeatable. And, never letting the facts get in the way of a good story, brags, "There is not a man around who can give me half a fight."

The Body served 17 years in the Navy, some in Vietnam. Like anyone who served in Nam, he went through hell, serving with the underwater demolition forces in life-or-death situations. He has now applied his training to the ring, making every one of his matches a life-or-death situation as well.

To date, Ventura's greatest accomplishment came when he teamed up with Adrian Adonis, an East-West tag team that combined the best of both worlds. The perfectly matched twosome proved their virtuosity—and, not incidentally, their superiority—by winning the AWA world tag team championship. Although Adonis and the Body no longer team together, they still harbor a hope that someday they will team up once again, bringing to such a team their own special skills and their mutual respect for each other.

When Ventura and Adonis toured the East, their charm and all-around appeal won them a full spread of publicity in *People* magazine. The article not only provided them with the

notoriety they sought, but provided Ventura with a forum for displaying his full-spread ego. "When you're as great as I am, success just seems to come naturally," he said.

Unfortunately, during his stay in the WWF areas Ventura could never win the championship. In several matches with champion Bob Backlund, Ventura came away empty-handed, unable to pin the champ or win the belt. In frustration, Ventura complained aloud that he had been "robbed," holding that he had the formidable Backlund beaten several times but that the all-American champion had always pulled some sort of stunt to hold on to his title. The Body even went so far as to accuse Backlund of hitting the referee intentionally to get himself disqualified, thereby retaining his belt on a technicality. In that particular match, held in New Jersey, Ventura was awarded the victory but not the coveted title, a moral victory that still galls him.

Ventura is convinced that someday he will be *the* champion, because, "I am too good not to be." It is a dream he has been following since he first turned professional in 1975. And although he has won the Pacific Northwest heavyweight championship, the Hawaiian heavyweight championship, the Hawaiian tag team championship, with Steve Strong, and the AWA tag team championship, he still craves *the* championship. And will go to any lengths to get it. And "no Body" doubts that!

Opposite: Jesse Ventura and "Mr. USA," Tony Atlas, in a battle of wills for the upper hand. Above: Ventura makes Steve "O" holler ooooh! with a side headlock.

NIKOLAI VOLKOFF

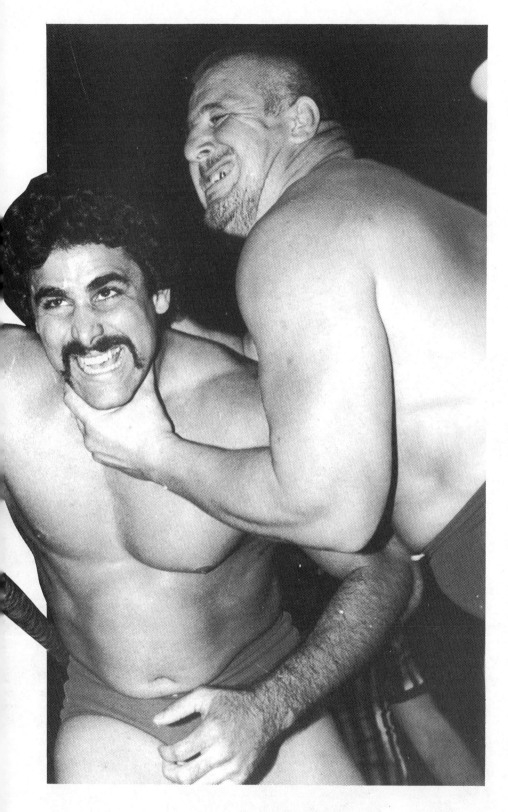

THIS BIG, BAD BEAR IS ONE of the toughest, meanest, baddest men on the wrestling landscape. Proclaiming Russian athletes to be the best athletes in the world, and himself to be "the greatest" of all Russian athletes, Nikolai Volkoff has gone to any, and many, lengths to show it. And to show those "soft" Americans who is boss.

Freddie Blassie was the person responsible for bringing this one-man wrecking crew onto the scene back in 1974. And from his first day Volkoff dedicated himself to a "win-at-any-cost" strategy, dealing out pain and terror to anyone who dared step in his way.

For four years Volkoff pursued the championship, but it eluded his territorial aggrandizement. Once he held the great Bruno Sammartino to a 54-minute draw. But the 11:00 curfew ended Volkoff's dreams of capturing the crown and subjugating Sammartino. In their return encounter the Living Legend soundly trounced the huge Volkoff.

Volkoff then voluntarily boycotted the wrestling scene, but he returned in 1976. This time, teaming up with Japan's Tor Kamata, Volkoff and company walked over, through, and around others, doing everything to them but grinding his

Nikolai Volkoff has Al Perez all chocked up.

144

hobnail boots into their throats. Then, inexplicably, he returned to Russia, his all-conquering ambitions seemingly quenched. In 1981 he came back yet again and, joining forces with Chris Markoff, finally won the crown that had always seemed to be just beyond his grasp: the tag team titles in both Florida and the Mid-Atlantic areas.

With a measure of success finally his, Volkoff tried his bullying tactics in other world venues, wrestling in Japan, Hong Kong, and Australia. And always with success. In July 1983 the huge Russian again returned to America, and is still here today. When asked why he had departed the ''land of the free and the home of the brave,'' the always ungracious Volkoff replied, ''I had grown weak and weary of being around nothing but American losers.'' He now gloats that he feels reborn by his trips home to Russia and that he will triumph over all as he challenges some of the biggest names in wrestling.

Believing that he will ''one day rule the world'' like his Russian ancestors, this huge 325-pound mountain of terror with the 65-inch chest, 24-inch neck, and 23-inch arms will do anything to make his boast come true!

This big, bad Russian plans to conquer the wrestling world.

ZAMBUIE EXPRESS

MR. ELIJAH AKEEM AND MR. Kareem Muhammed make quite an imposing team. These two "brothers" are as big and as bad as they come. Although they have been friends for years, they never actually wrestled as a team until Kevin Sullivan brought them together. Sullivan convinced the 6-foot 2-inch, 310-pound Elijah Akeem and the 6-foot 4-inch, 340-pound Muhammed to give togetherness a try. While under Kevin Sullivan's influence, the Zambuie Express, as they became known, captured the Global tag team title from Scott McGhee and Mike Graham, and they were well on their way to fame and fortune.

"We owe a great deal to Kevin Sullivan," Akeem stated. "If it weren't for his wisdom and guidance, we wouldn't be in the position we are in today." Sullivan was forced to leave Florida, however, after losing a "loser leave town" bout against Dusty Rhodes, and turned the Zambuie Express over to Gentleman Jim Holiday.

"I made them what they are today," brags the Gentleman.

"Before I came on the scene they were good, but now they are great. The Zambuie Express will go down in history as the greatest tag team ever to grace the squared circle."

Although Jim Holiday speaks highly of the Express, they do not speak so highly of him. "No man tells us what to do," says Elijah Akeem when questioned about their relationship with Holiday. "Me and Kareem can fight our own battles, sign our own contracts, and make our own money without any help from anyone. If you want to

Kareem Muhammed backs Butch Miller into the corner—and into trouble.

146

The Zambuie Express, Kareem Muhammed and Elijah Akeem.

know anything, don't ask it behind our backs. We will give you the answer you need to hear.''

''That's right,'' adds Kareem Muhammed.

Aside from their dissension with Holiday, the vicious duo have involved themselves in a raging feud against Black Jack Mulligan and Dusty Rhodes. After the Zambuie Express captured the US tag team title in a tournament in New Mexico, they returned to the Sunshine State a team possessed. They barreled over everyone placed

in their path, and in the process they began a vicious feud with Black Jack Mulligan that shook the state.

Mulligan has battled with the Express in both single and tag team matches, and every one of their bouts has turned out to be a bloody brawl. ''I won't be satisfied until I drive that revolutionary army out of here,'' proclaims Mulligan. ''They've been messing with me for too long now, and I can't stand it. Look, I'm going to put some hurting on those two. I don't know who they think they're

messing with, but those two fools and their slimy manager, Jim Holiday, will get what is coming to them.''

But the 650 pounds of sheer terror aren't too worried. There may be teams equally as vicious, but no one has the ferociousness and sheer brutality of the Zambuie Express. They have made a name for themselves, a name that sends shivers up the backs of would-be opponents. Chances are that they will stay on top for a long time. The Zambuie connection is surely a force to watch in the future.

LARRY ZBYSZKO

Larry Zbyszko stretches Bruno Sammartino, Jr., from A to Z.

Tommy Rich receives the side of Zbyszko's foot—and then some—in a side kick.

LARRY ZBYSZKO STYLES HIM-self the "New Living Legend," a self-serving title that has made skeptics throughout most of the wrestling world sneer. Larry seems to be carrying around a ten-pound chip on his shoulder. No doubt it is becoming heavier by the day, too, because most of the top names in the sport refuse to wrestle him. Larry can have a mean, bad attitude when it suits his purpose. He claims that big names won't wrestle with him because "they know I'm their master."

Zbyszko has only himself to blame for his bad reputation. His attitude first manifested it-self when he attacked Bruno Sammartino on television and began one of the most bitter feuds ever. Ironically, Zbyszko was trained by Bruno, who treated him like a son. Larry be-came an excellent grappler; the career of the new star began to soar; but something continually gnawed away at Larry, and that was that wherever he went the public was always comparing him to Bruno. For someone with a huge ego and unlimited ambitions this was unaccepta-ble. Larry couldn't stand not be-ing number one!

So, one wretchedly morbid night Larry and Bruno fought it out in Shea Stadium. It was a sight the ancient Romans would have enjoyed. The two wres-tlers attacked each other in a steel-cage match in front of 40,000 fans. This was the night Larry crowned himself the New Living Legend.

Shortly afterward Bruno re-tired. Larry next fought a grue-some battle against champion Bob Backlund, and although Larry won the match, he did not win the title—the rules of cham-pionship matches specify that the champion must be pinned or submit in order to lose his

belt, which Larry failed to do.

Larry was unable to get the championship bouts he craved so much, so he signed up with the International Wrestling Or-ganization. He became involved in a vicious series of battles all over the East Coast against Bruno's son, Sammartino, Jr.

Larry's attitude darkened dur-ing these bouts. He claimed that Bruno, Jr., was "steamed" at him because he was superior to

Zbyszko tosses Sammartino, Jr.

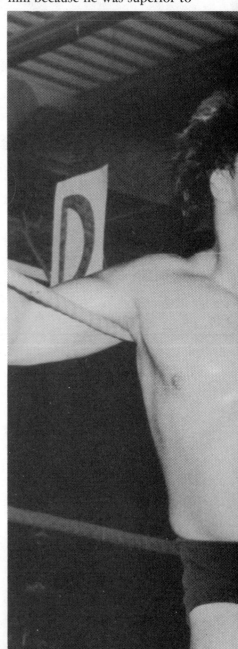

his dad. Larry said he wanted to teach Bruno, Jr., a lesson. However, the bouts clearly indicated that Bruno, Jr., has the "stuff" to be around for years. Nevertheless, Larry still clung to his claim as the New Living Legend.

Marching straight into the World Championship Wrestling area, Zbyszko arrogantly asserted to the world that "someone's got to be the world heavyweight champion . . . and it might as well be me!" He challenged Paul Orndorff but was denied a match. Zbyszko's anger turned to fury when Killer Brooks was granted a match with Orndorff. Infuriated and desperate, Zbyszko made an offer to Brooks that he couldn't refuse: "Beat Mr. Wonderful and turn the belt over to me, and I'll give you twenty-five thousand dollars." Brooks beat Orndorff and, in an un-precedented move, turned the belt over to Zbyszko.

Amid cries of "Foul play!" Zbyszko firmly stood his ground and responded, "I did what I had to do." And then he added, "Anyone who wants the belt can have it . . . if they beat me!"

Larry Zbyszko is indeed a living legend, even if he did create the legend in a somewhat unusual fashion.

THE UGLY

ABDULLAH THE BUTCHER

MOST SAY WRESTLING'S A sport; a few call it a spectacle. But one man sees it as an arena of madness, mayhem, and the macabre. That man is known throughout the world as Abdullah the Butcher.

Originally hailing from the country of Sudan, Abdullah first introduced his brand of wrestling terror to the western world in Canada. Abdullah's thirst for new blood and his nomadic heritage led him to the squared circle of the National Wrestling Federation soon thereafter. The fact that the NWF title was soon his seemed secondary to the fear and madness that Abdullah wrought upon his opponents and wrestling fans alike.

Still, the wanderlust that consumed this savage 400-pound giant from the Sudan would not rest, and once again Abdullah was called to wage war in other foreign lands, including Japan and Trinidad. Abdullah's time in Japan was spent wrestling such local idols as Antonio Inoki, the Giant Baba, and Tasumi Fujinami, all three of whom were smashed beneath the might of this massive madman. Yet, when opponents' heads turn in the direction of this behemoth, it is always with reverence and admiration.

Awesome is one word that comes to mind when one tries to convey the savagery and sickness of an Abdullah match. This was especially true of his battle with Carlos Colon, a near riot that saw police jump into the fray to control the mob. And fans from Florida won't soon forget the havoc Abdullah brought to the Sunshine State a few years back. But all of that was garden-variety brutality compared to the savagery Abdullah brought with him to Houston the night he wrestled Scott Casey. No one who was there that grizzly night will ever again see—or wish to see—mayhem of the sort that ensued that infamous evening. Abdullah launched a surprise attack on the popular cowboy, and within minutes Casey's blood poured freely about the ring. Terry Funk rushed into the ring to rescue Casey from this demonic devastation, but Abdullah, possessed with an inhuman desire for blood, pulled a fork and mauled Funk so badly that Terry was sidelined for three important matches.

Frequent arrests for violence—both in and out of the ring—the foreign objects that are in evidence during almost every match, and shredding animals with his teeth are all part of Abdullah's mad antics. This man can only be described as "too sick." His onetime manager Hugo Savinovitch says, "Abdullah's idea of success is not measured by a title belt but by the amount of pain he inflicts in the ring. Besides, Abdullah feels that all his opponents are beneath him." Unfortunately, most wind up that way!

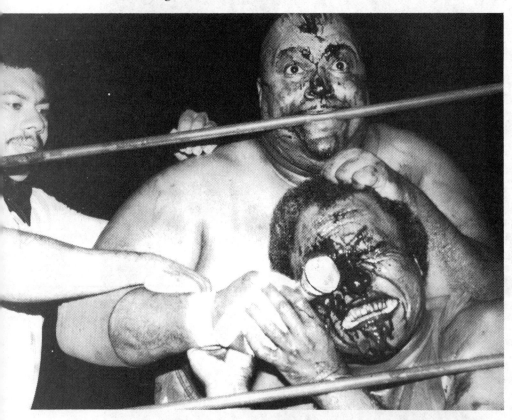

Above: Abdullah uses a foreign object to etch pain in the face of Carlos Colon. Opposite: "Jumbo" Tommy Tsuruta and Antonio Inoki bookend Abdullah in a volume that bespeaks chapters on the Butcher's horror.

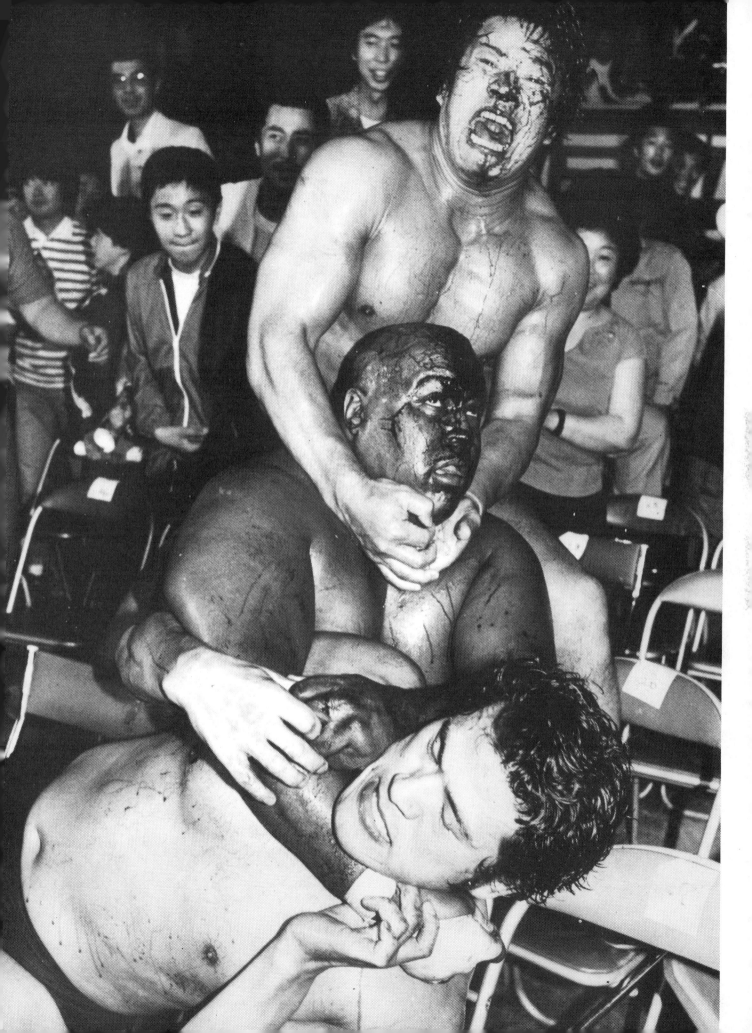

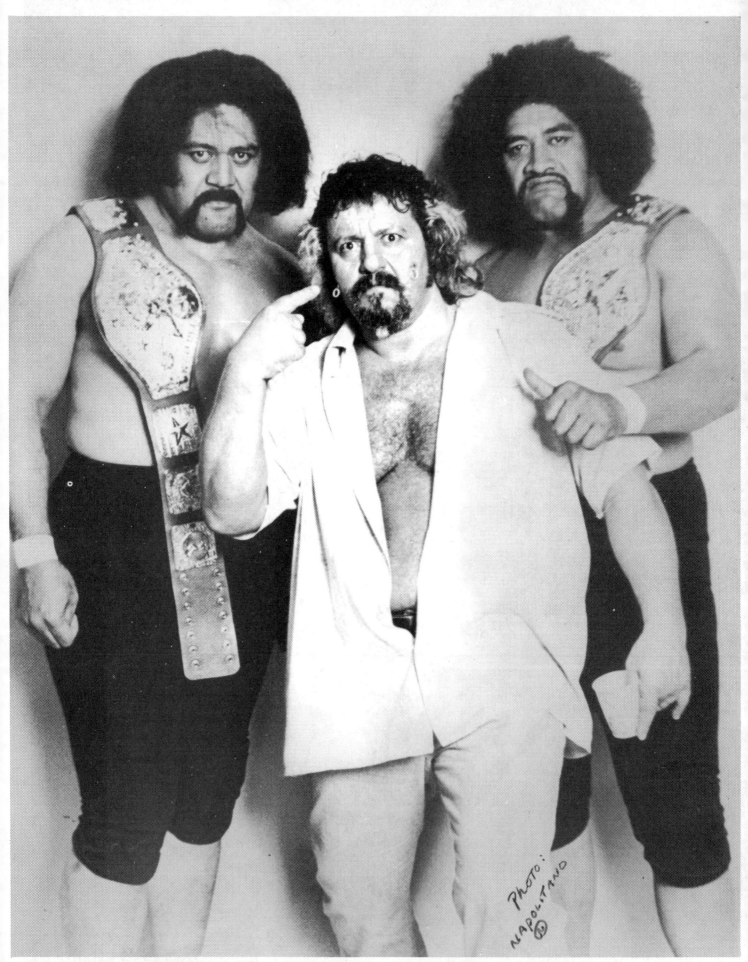

"Captain" Lou Albano caught with the Wild Samoans, Afa and Sika, in a friendlier moment.

LOU ALBANO

"CAPTAIN" LOU ALBANO HAS been a major character in the wrestling world for nearly 25 years. Today the Captain is respectfully referred to as "the manager of champions." No other manager in the history of the sport has guided more men to the championship than Lou Albano.

Ivan Koloff, "the Russian Bear," was the Captain's first protégé to make it big. While under the Captain's guidance, Koloff defeated the "Living Legend," Bruno Sammartino, to capture the WWF title. The Mongols were the Captain's first tag team champions, and it has been in the tag team division that the Captain has truly excelled. The teams that Albano has guided to tag team championship status include Tarzan Tyler and Crazy Luke Graham, King Curtis and Baron Scicluan, the Valiants (twice), the Masked Executioners, the Yukon Lumberjacks, the Samoans (three times), the Moondogs, and Mr. Fuji and Mr. Saito. Besides, Albano also has managed the Magnificent Muraco during his long reign as Intercontinental champion.

Lou Albano has usually been more controversial than his protégés. It seems that whenever Lou Albano becomes involved in something, a major explosion occurs. He has not mellowed with age and is even wilder and crazier than ever. He is always on the lookout for new fields to conquer, and his latest endeavor is in the rock video field.

He teamed up with rock star Cyndi Lauper, anxious to be of help in making her into a superstar. They put together the rock video "Girls Just Want to Have Fun," featuring Cyndi Lauper. In the video Albano plays the part of Cyndi's father and acts just like he does when he is

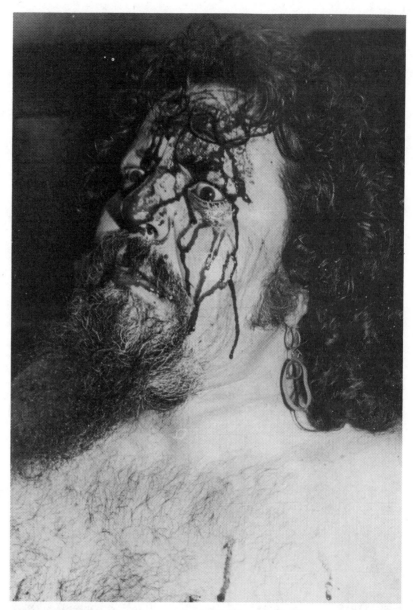

"The Captain," Lou Albano, one of the most influential men in wrestling for over 25 years.

managing one of his own protégés. "I'm trying to straighten her out," explains Albano. "I tell her, 'You got to do it this way,' and she says, 'But, Daddy, that's the way it's got to be because girls just want to have fun.' "

When asked how she felt about working with the Captain, Ms. Lauper replied, "I found Lou Albano very professional, and it is such a thrill for me to work with a person with such a level of expertise. Working with Lou has changed my outlook on everything. He's the best, and I only want to be associated with the best."

Lou Albano is definitely one of the most influential men in wrestling. Like him or not, during his illustrious career he has done it all. In his wrestling days the Captain held the world tag team championship as part of a team known as the Sicilians, with partner Tony Altamore; he has managed a WWF heavyweight champion, an Intercontinental champion, and numerous tag team champions. But he's not finished yet. Lou Albano has promised to guide many more men—and perhaps a few ladies—to stardom in the near future.

OX BAKER

The Ox digs his knuckles into the features of what used to be the Invader.

FOR THE PAST 17 YEARS BIG, Bad Ox Baker has terrorized the wrestling scene. At 6 feet 5 inches and 300 pounds, he is as big as an ox and twice as tough. He has heart-punched his way to many victories all over the world, and lately the nasty brute has been spreading havoc in the Caribbean. "They told me there was stiff competition there," growled the Ox, "but I'm still waiting to hear who they were talking about."

The Ox can actually be rather charming outside the ring, but when he steps into the squared circle, he is all business. Dirty business. His goal is to win—at any cost. He may not dazzle with speed or technical wrestling maneuvers, but he gets the job done, and that's what really matters. "Hey," explains the Ox, "it's a lot easier to kick someone or even choke him than to put an arm bar on him, and besides, it's even more ef-

fective. In my career I've been able to survive because of my ability to absorb punishment and to dish out pain."

As soon as Ox Baker arrived on the Caribbean scene he found himself involved in a raging controversy with the local favorite, the Invader. "He warned me to stay out of his way," recalls the Ox. "That was his first mistake! Several weeks later he stepped into the ring against me. He tried his silly moves, slipped, and landed on the canvas. I drew back my foot and knocked the wind out of him, and while he tried to catch his breath, I threw some murderous heart punches! Crack went his ribs! It was great! The people were crying when their hero had to be carried out on a stretcher. From that moment on I've been the toast of Puerto Rico and the rest of the Caribbean islands, too."

It is true that the Invader was put out of action for six weeks after absorbing the Ox's vicious heart punches. But he did return for revenge several months later. "He may think he got back at me, but where is the Invader today? He had something hidden in his fist in that return match, and that is the only way he was able even to enter the ring against me without shaking in terror. But he couldn't hurt the Ox. And where is he today? The last I heard he was chopping down sugar cane in one of the islands close to Florida."

Baker's claim that the Invader had something hidden in his fist is quite interesting, for the same claim has been made against the Ox himself numerous times. But the Ox has always denied that it was true. "Why should the master of the heart punch put something in my fist? The only thing you feel when you get hit with an Ox Baker heart punch is my

Ox Baker gores the head of Carlos Colon in a side headlock.

sheer power. The Invader was a mediocre wrestler in the States before he came to the Caribbean. He almost became a legend here by copying my heart punch. But he had to put something in his fist to give him the power to be a tough guy. When I showed up his charade was over.

"I have to give credit to Stan Stasiak, though. At one time he was the number-one heart puncher, but, unfortunately, he didn't have the viciousness to drive two, three, four heart punches in succession into his opponent. He would lay one in and then back off. That's not my style. I go for broke. Only when my opponent is flat on the mat do I stop, and then I'll give him one more for good measure."

There is no one quite like Ox Baker. No one matches his viciousness, his joy in injuring his opponents. Ox Baker will undoubtedly continue his brutal ways for many years.

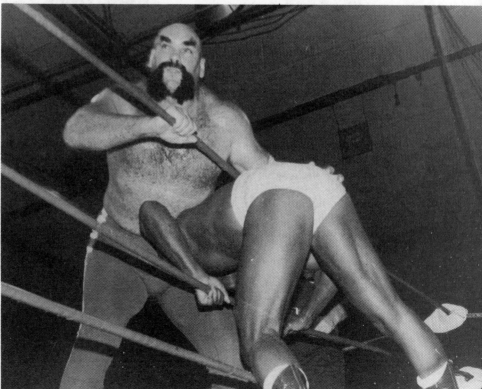

Ox has his opponent trapped helplessly in the yoke of the ropes.

THE GREAT KABUKI

THE MYSTICAL POWERS OF the Great Kabuki have wreaked havoc and horror wherever he has appeared on the wrestling scene. Kabuki's past is as mysterious as the green mist that emanates from his mouth. He comes from Singapore, we do know that much, and he weighs in at 238 pounds of mysterious and awesome power. Another thing known for certain about the Great Kabuki is that he is one of the most feared wrestlers in the sport today.

"Kabuki's power will never be understood," claims manager Gary Hart. "I have been with him for a long time and seen so much, but many of the things he does still surprise me. You just can never overestimate his powers. Just when you think you have the man figured out, he comes up with a new move to baffle his opponents. In all my years in the sport, I've never, ever encountered anyone quite like the Great Kabuki. Others may try to mimic his style, but for Kabuki this is his way of life. He is the real thing, and I shudder to think what would happen if Kabuki ever encountered an impostor."

During his career the Great Kabuki has wrestled all over the world, always with the same devastating results. He has managed to capture the Texas heavyweight title during his travels and will no doubt be adding more such honors to his mysterious résumé. He is famous for his side karate kicks, his martial arts expertise, and the mysterious green mist that he spits into his opponents' eyes. With this combination as well as the ever-present threat of the unexpected, Kabuki is a most dangerous man. He is a mystery man to be feared.

Kabuki pats Junkyard Dog in his own affectionate manner, fingers first.

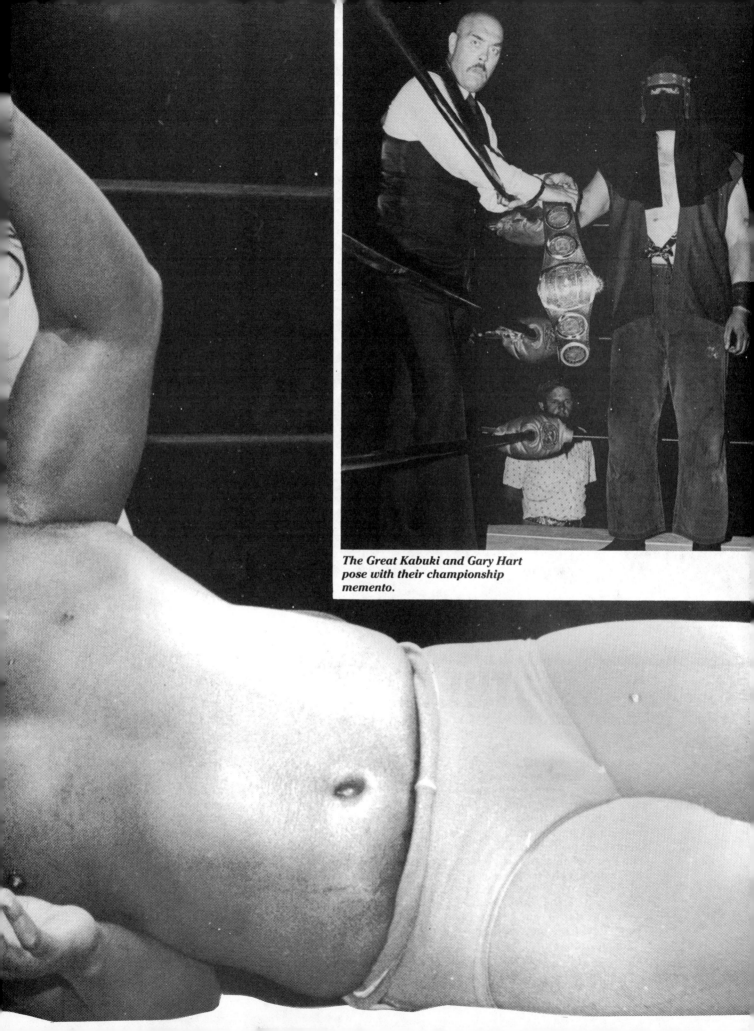

The Great Kabuki and Gary Hart pose with their championship memento.

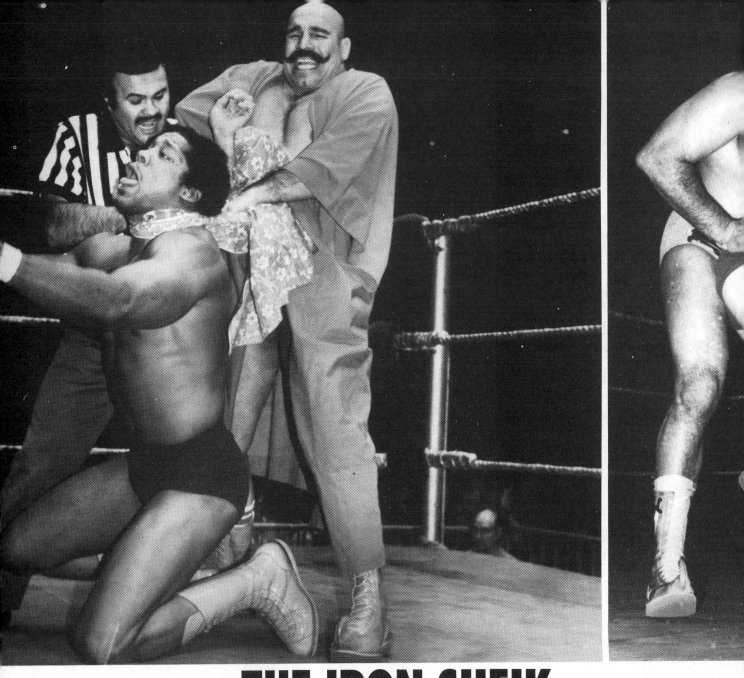

THE IRON SHEIK

THIS MADMAN FROM IRAN has spread his wrath, hatred, and devastation on all the unsuspecting wrestlers throughout the wrestling world. Although the Iron Sheik has a habit of making up his own rules, he also has an excellent wrestling background, having represented Iran in the 1972 Munich Olympic Games, where he won a gold medal. He has also competed in the Pan American Games, the Asian Games, and the European Games as well. The Iron Sheik is the first Iranian professional wrestler to compete in the Unites States.

The Sheik has wrestled all over the world, as well, and has held many titles, including the Canadian heavyweight, the European heavyweight, the WWF, the Asian, and the Mid-Atlantic belts. His greatest claim to fame, however, was winning the WWF title from Bob Backlund in December 1983. During his career the Iranian has wrestled in the WWF, the NWA, and the AWA territories and holds victories over the biggest and the best in the business. He has defeated such outstanding wrestlers as Tito Santana, "Captain Redneck" Dick Murdock,

Tommy Rich, Tony "Mr. USA" Atlas, and Bob Backlund.

Before coming to the WWF, the Iron Sheik was headquartered in San Antonio, Texas, and often wrestled as a tag team partner with Sheepherder Luke Williams. He also wrestled in the Georgia area, where he was the National TV champion and tag partner of Ivan Koloff, another of Freddie "Ayatollah" Blassie's charges.

Why did Fred Blassie, an American who became wealthy in this country, hook up with this Iranian madman? Why would Blassie take to dressing

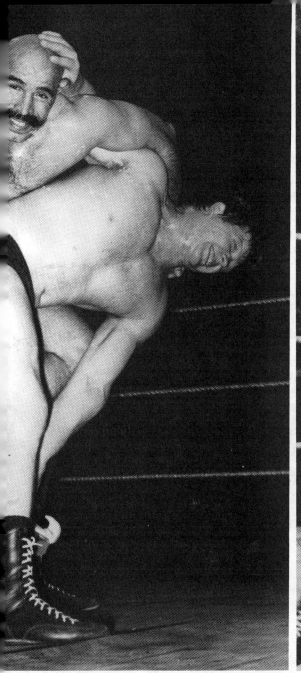

himself like an Iranian and calling himself Ayatollah to manage the Sheik? The answer is simple: he knows the hate, the hunger, and the desire that drives this madman. He knows about the Sheik's abilities and experiences. The Iron Sheik's mission, simply stated, is to cripple, humble, and humiliate all the weak Americans and to prove, once and for all, his superiority and the superiority of his people by giving them the world championship belt. True to his mission, the Iron Sheik delivered on this promise when he defeated Bob Backlund to win the WWF title. Although his reign was short-lived, the Iron Sheik still managed to win this

prestigious honor.

The Sheik is amazingly strong. He has offered thousands of dollars to anyone who can swing his exercise clubs—and no one has ever succeeded. His wrestling skills are equally amazing, and he has developed several new holds, including a submission hold in which he sits on his opponent's back and pulls back on his neck. He calls this unique hold his cobra clutch, but it is quite different from Sergeant Slaughter's version—and many wrestlers feel it may be the more dangerous of the two.

Yet another of the Iron Sheik's weapons is one that a wrestler can only possess after

years of ring warfare: experience with a capital E—his own as well as that of his manager, Ayatollah Blassie.

American wrestlers—Bob Backlund, Dusty Rhodes, Sergeant Slaughter, Junkyard Dog, Tito Santana, and the rest—*beware!* The Sheik is someone to be reckoned with.

Opposite left: The Iron Sheik tries to gift wrap Tony Atlas with a strangle hold. Center: The Iron Sheik has Bob Backlund in an abdominal stretch. Right: Tito Santana and the Iron Sheik struggle to get the upper hand—and the upper everything else.

KAMALA

THIS MONSTROUS MAN FROM Uganda weighs in at 360 pounds of sheer terror. Kamala is one of the most unusual, if not the most frightening, men in wrestling today. He is big, black, and paints his bald head in an African design. He wears an African warrior-type skirt that barely covers his bulging blubber, and all in all he resembles a very successful cannibal. He has a habit of diving on his opponents from the ring posts, squashing the unsuspecting competitors into submission.

He is powerful and dangerous, and in combination with his ever-present Friday, he is total destruction. "That's right," crows former manager Scandor Akbar. "Kamala is one of my main men in Devastation, Inc. He is unusual—to say the least—and he follows orders well. He does exactly what I tell him to do. Together we have been very successful. We have already run Bruiser Brody out of town, destroyed the Great Kabuki, and demolished the so-called Giant, Andre. Kamala is without a doubt the most powerful man in wrestling today. He is not afraid to take whatever steps are necessary to hurt, maim, or cripple our opponents. He is true Devastation in its purest form."

Kamala has been wrestling professionally for several years and has appeared in Tennessee, the Mid South, the World Class territory, and the WWF—always with the same devastating results. Wherever he goes, he is destined to bring along havoc and destruction to the wrestling scene.

Opposite: Kamala and Scandor Akbar in their Most Wanted shot.
Above: Kamala has Adrian Street right on target.

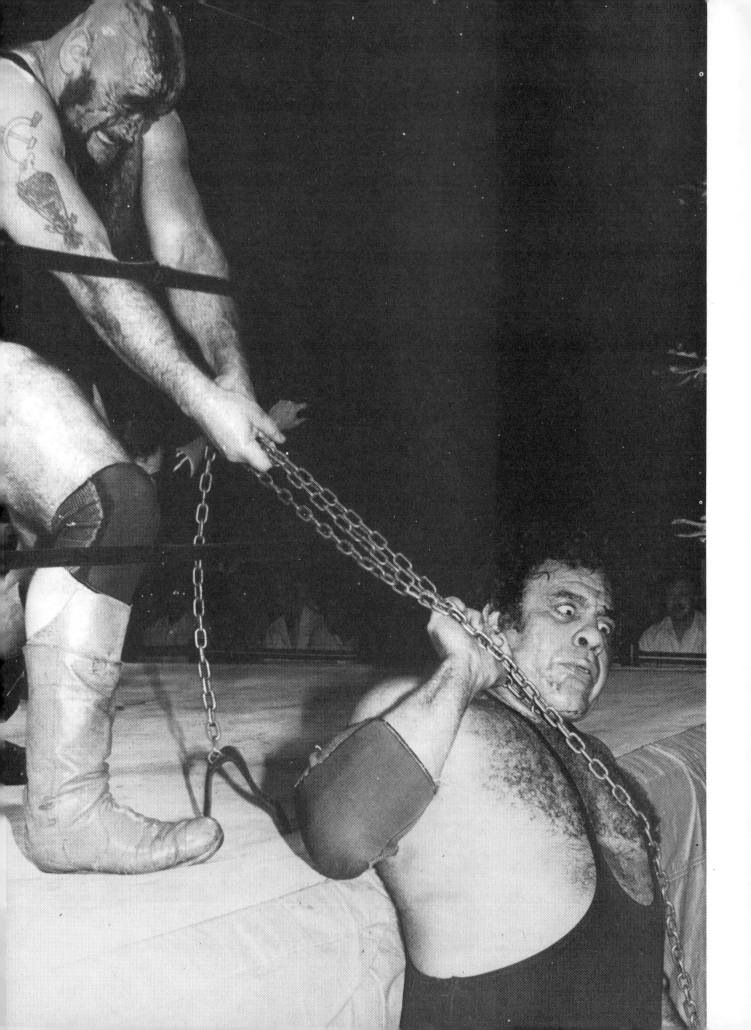

IVAN KOLOFF

SINCE ITS BEGINNING, THE so-called Cold War between the Soviet Union and the United States has been a stalemate, involving much talk and very little action. However, one man has assumed the responsibility for keeping it alive and, in the course of so doing, displaying Soviet superiority at all costs. His arena is not that of Europe or the Mideast but rather in rings all across America. We're speaking of wrestling's Russian threat, Ivan Koloff, the Russian Bear.

Koloff's sordid career took him from behind the Iron Curtain and into the American limelight some 15 years ago. In that time Ivan has met wrestling's best. Weighing over 260 pounds, he has used his speed and mastery to roll over Dusty Rhodes (their many confrontations are always total warfare), break Captain Redneck, and even defeat wrestling's favorite son, Bruno Sammartino. That moment in the spotlight was indeed a brief one for Ivan as he was soon defeated by Pedro Morales and lost the belt he had taken from Bruno.

Whether wrestling alone or in tag teams with men like Chris Markoff, or Don Kernodle, or his nephew, Nikita, the demonic Ivan will go to any lengths to win—which is also why the unruly Russian is not exactly a fan favorite. His rough maneuvers and questionable tactics have earned him the epithets *sneak, coward,* and *cheat.* Whatever he is, Koloff is a very tough competitor and one with an impressive string of titles trailing behind him.

The championship has been and always will be Koloff's goal in wrestling. It is on his mind constantly, and his oftentimes illegal maneuvers are intended only to bring him closer to that goal. And he has achieved his goal on many occasions. He has captured the Georgia state championship, the Georgia tag team belt, the WWF heavyweight title, the Florida championship, as well as many European titles.

Known as one of the most vicious grapplers by both fans and opponents, Koloff is honored by his reputation. In his matches he uses all but the proverbial hammer and sickle to defeat his opponents. His favorite type of warfare is the Russian chain match, a brutal throwback to battles of yesteryear in which Koloff and his opponent are chained to each other and go to war until one is soundly defeated and carried off.

Although Koloff admits that it's not right to break the rules, he's not opposed to breaking them in order to win. His objective is to win—whatever the cost.

Koloff is at ease in the ring and believes that Russians are stronger and better trained than other wrestlers. His kicks are known as being especially vicious, but he denies the accusations that he hides anything in his boots. "I wear heavy boots," he says defensively. "They weigh four pounds apiece. And I do have a mean kick—but that's because I'm so strong."

He keeps his incredible strength up to par by training with weights every day. He has a split routine, six days a week, and he runs every second day for three or four miles. That is the secret to his skill—natural ability and training, plus a desire to win that is not inflexible when it comes to the rules.

Today NATO needn't worry about this Russian Bear; that's left to the American fans and Koloff's combatants. Koloff currently claims, "I'm in the best shape of my life. I wish to

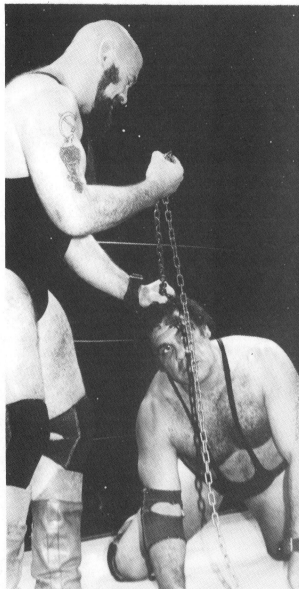

Opposite: Ivan Koloff makes Angelo Mosca, Sr., see red. Above: Koloff tries to subjugate Mosca with his own form of the Iron Curtain.

regain the WWF title and dance through Red Square with the belt high over my head!'' Coming from a man who doesn't know the meaning of *détente,* the public should heed the warning and take his threats seriously, not with a grain of SALT.

LeDuc tries to "get his man," Dick Slater, as Jack Brisco watches from outside the ring.

JOE LeDUC

FOR THIRTEEN YEARS JOE Le-Duc has been traveling around the wrestling world, and everywhere he has appeared, the rugged lumberjack has left his mark. The talented Canadian has captured the Southeastern heavyweight title, the Southern heavyweight title, the Maritime championship, Canadian heavyweight championship, Mid-Atlantic title, and Mid-Atlantic TV title, as well as numerous other titles and awards.

Although the Canadian is just as often booed as cheered, depending on the crowd, he claims that he never changes his style. "The people are fickle," he says. "One time they love you, and the next time they hate you." But no matter what the crowd thinks, Joe LeDuc is always rough and rugged.

In the past LeDuc has feuded with Dick Slater, the One Man Gang, and every other wrestler in the H & H stable. But LeDuc's main problem centers around his treatment by former manager Sir Oliver Humperdink. "He really played me dirty," claims LeDuc. "He stole my money and left me high and dry. But I got back at him. Now he knows better than to ever mess with Joe LeDuc."

And so does Slater. Slater and LeDuc were stable mates of Humperdink's, and when Le-Duc left the stable, Humperdink instructed Slater to get rid of Le-Duc. But no matter how hard Slater has tried, he still has not

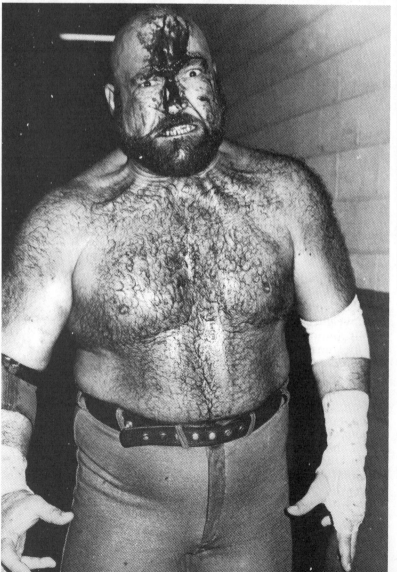

been able to finish off the tough lumberjack. "Imagine Humperdink sending someone as weak as Dick Slater to get rid of me," laughs LeDuc. "The man is simply not in my league. I proved that in Richmond when I captured his Mid-Atlantic TV title in a lumberjack match. In fact, I've never been defeated in a lumberjack match and I never will."

Of all specialty matches, the Canadian lumberjack match could be the roughest in the

The menacing face of Joe LeDuc.

sport. LeDuc himself explains, "In a lumberjack match you have to be ready for anything. There are no rules, and the first man who can knock the other out cold is the winner." There are also men positioned on the outside of the ring to bodily return a contestant who decides to try to make a fast exit. At times these enforcers are even equipped with whips with which to beat a yellow wrestler back into the ring.

You have to be tough to survive that, and "tough" is LeDuc's middle name. He is truly "king" of the lumberjack match, and his incredible record in this type of match backs up his claim. He has defeated Jerry Lawler, Ron Fuller, Robert Fuller, Austin Idol, Paul Jones, Jimmy Valiant, Dino Bravo, and just about every star who has dared to enter such a match with him.

Recently, LeDuc has been wrestling mainly in single bouts, but there was a time when he and brother Paul were invincible as a tag team. Unfortunately, an injury to Paul caused the brothers to break up their act, and Joe has been on his own ever since.

"I've had a few good partners over the years," states LeDuc, "but no one could match up to my brother Paul."

With his sheer brutality and take-charge attitude, Canadian lumberjack Joe LeDuc shows no sign of slipping from his lofty position on wrestling's ladder of success for a long time.

THE DREAD NINJA WARRIOR, Kendo Nagasaki, inspires fear and dread in the hearts of opponent and fan alike. Creating a little hammock of havoc wherever he goes, Nagasaki has been seen in all parts of the world. His style is not one easily forgotten.

When Nagasaki enters the arena, electricity hangs heavily over the crowd. Painting his face in garish colors and designs, this ninja heavy matches his facial expressions with devilish physical ones as he executes dervishlike spins and twirls that seem almost superhuman. Most disturbing to the fans and, in particular, his opponents, is his constant use of illegal karate moves and foreign objects—like the long kendo sticks he uses to batter opponents.

Nagasaki's manager, J. J. Dillon, attributes many of his wrestler's maneuvers to the man's background and his language problem—Kendo speaks no English. Dillon argues that certain moves, looked upon here as illegal, are, in reality, a natural reflex for Kendo. But even Dillon cannot totally control his charge. Nagasaki's intensely competitive spirit sometimes gets the best of him and drives him almost to total frenzy.

Nagasaki's match with Black Jack Mulligan was a match in mayhem, one never to be for-

Kendo Nagasaki leaps off ropes onto the helpless form of El Gran Apollo.

KENDO NAGASAKI

gotten. Two kendo sticks were placed in the center of the ring. At the bell, whomever could reach them first was permitted to use them against his opponent. Mulligan was there first and grabbed them, but Nagasaki was able to gain them back in the infighting, and he used them unmercifully to crack open Black Jack's skull. The referee had to intervene to save Mulligan from serious, even fatal, injuries.

Kendo Nagasaki is something of a mystery. He does not speak to reporters and stays away from crowds and other wrestlers. Dillon claims that Kendo is uncomfortable with others and knows and trusts very few people. Dillon somehow survives as his associate by respecting both his wrestler and his privacy. But even Dillon, who tries to understand the Oriental mind of his wrestler, sometimes has difficulty fathoming why Nagasaki uses his karate in a manner totally opposed to the philosophy underlying the martial arts—offensively and not defensively, when it is not a graceful form of self-defense but a maiming and crippling agent.

Dillon believes the fans do not appreciate Kendo Nagasaki. And perhaps in this he's right. It's hard to really appreciate a man who is hell-bent on destruction in an ugly manner.

Nagasaki works his fingers to the bones of Barry Windham.

Above: Luke Williams salutes Bobby Jaggers with a flag of his native New Zealand. Opposite: Luke Williams and Butch Miller "pretty up" for a shot.

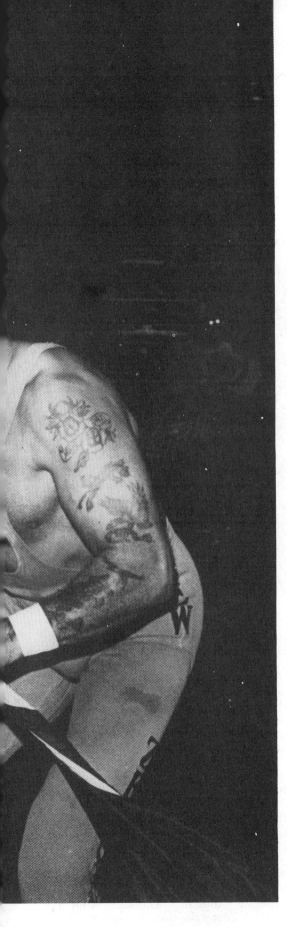

THE SHEEPERDERS

IF YOU'VE EVER HEARD THE Iron Sheik interviewed, you probably think that there is no put-down or degrading statement about our country or citizens to which you've not been subjected. Well, then, you haven't heard the Sheepherders. These rugged cousins, "Crazy" Luke Williams, "Wild" Butch Miller, and "Maniac" Jonathan Boyd, have spread their outrageous style of ring warfare from their homes in New Zealand to the isles of the South Pacific, the Caribbean, and to Canada. And lately they've haunted the rings of America. "Wild" Butch has stated more than once, "We want to teach these American wimps respect for the men of New Zealand. We're aiming to put our country at the forefront of your weak American minds. . . . That's where it rightfully belongs."

One American mind in which the Sheepherders' name and message has definitely been placed is "Hangman" Bobby Jaggers's. Jaggers joined forces with the Sheepherders and thereafter won more matches than he had ever dreamed possible. The Hangman felt that the Sheepherders had nothing to do with his success and soon parted company with them. Following their rupture, Jaggers tore up a New Zealand flag in front of millions of wrestling fans on the USA Cable Network.

Jonathan Boyd watched this insult to his country from a hospital bed, where he claims he was convalescing from injuries sustained as a result of Jaggers forcing his car off the road in a near-fatal crash. Boyd nevertheless dragged himself from his hospital bed to make the proclamation, "This is war! We will import the toughest, roughest wrestlers to Texas to take care of Jaggers and his wetback friend Buddy Moreno."

The Iron Sheik soon came to Texas to help his friend's threat come to fruition, and Jaggers and Moreno paid the price. Later, Luke Williams and Bobby Jaggers met in a wild match that left Jaggers with two broken arms, severe lacerations of the head, and several cracked ribs. The message was clear: Don't get these wild men angry!

Wild antics, which led to riots in Boston, are combined with scientific skill and technique to make mutton out of all the "dirty American dogs and slimy wetbacks" who cross the Sheepherders' path. In terms of future opponents, Luke says, "Bring those worthless Americans on . . . We're the master race and aim to prove it. Any greaser who says otherwise, we'll light up like a Christmas tree!"

GEORGE "THE ANIMAL" STEELE

"The Animal" on the loose.

THERE IS ONLY ONE TRUE Animal in this sport, and that is, of course, George Steele. He bears a close resemblance to the prehistoric Neanderthal man and can only be described as the wildest, the craziest, the most insane wrestler ever to enter the ring.

Unlike wine, George Steele has not mellowed with age. He has been on the wrestling scene for quite a while, and if anything, he is even more abusive than when he began. Don't expect to see many legitimate wrestling maneuvers in a Steele match. He doesn't use them. He may surprise the audience occasionally with a true wrestling move, but his usual style consists of biting, kicking, stomping, chewing, and mauling. The Animal has been highly successful using these unorthodox techniques, but many good wrestlers have suffered terribly from his abuse.

Should a beast like this be allowed to compete in the sport? He has actually been barred from competing in their territory by many athletic commissions, and his blatant use of illegal tactics has left him with few friends among the commissioners, not to mention his poor opponents.

And not only do his opponents suffer—the referees who are right there in the line of fire have quite a time trying to keep this beast under control. "He's the worst," claims New York referee Al Vass. "I've been in the ring with that man many times, and I've never seen a crazier wrestler. I never know if he even understands me when I tell him to break a hold. He just looks at you with those rolling eyes and starts grunting and groaning like a rhinoceros in heat. Refereeing a George Steele match is like being trapped in a cage with a rabid St. Bernard."

If the referees feel this way, imagine how his opponents must feel as this wild man enters the ring. The Animal has battered both Bruno Sammartino and Bob Backlund with the WWF title at stake. Fortunately for Backlund, Sammartino, and the fans, the Animal did not have success against either of the two champions: in each instance it was his wildness that was his undoing.

George Steele has invaded the East four times, first under the management of the Grand Wizard, next with "Captain" Lou Albano, then with Fred Blassie, and finally Mr. Fuji. But no matter who manages this madman, his tactics never change. He is evil, calculating, and downright doglike in his attacks.

His physical makeup is enough to send an opponent running. His head is completely bald, and his hairy body resembles that of a grizzly bear. Whenever he is perturbed, his eyes point skyward and his green tongue curls up. The man is unbelievable.

Bruno Sammartino has said of the Animal, "That man is crazy. I've faced big men, strong men, many powerful men in my career, but I've never been up against anyone as crazy and wild as George Steele. Looking back, I would have to rate him right up there as one of my toughest opponents."

Animal, Animal, Animal. That's the only way to describe George Steele.

George "the Animal" Steele corners Pepe Figueroa.

ADRIAN STREET

WHEN YOU THINK OF PRO-fessional wrestling, chances are that massive, tough, and even downright mean and vicious men come to mind. Shopping trips to Paris, a taste for frozen vanilla daiquiries, and a need to be sure one's hair and makeup are neat have no place in the life of the typical wrestler. But no one ever claimed Adrian Street was typical, only extremely exotic.

The Exotic One's career began in England at the ripe old age of 16. "The artist in my soul was screaming for some type of expression," remembers the man known as Adrian Street. "Of course, my family wanted this to take a more conventional path. But school bored me, so I opted for the 'barbaric' world of wrestling. I'd never been beat and figured this was my calling. I'd bring art to this dark realm."

Adrian's natural ring prowess and artistic showmanship landed him in the States. Accompanied by his ever-present personal valet, Miss Linda, Adrian soon became the Boy George of the wrestling world, introducing his own brand of "culture" to American fans and ring opponents, who were handpicked on the basis of their class and couth.

But measuring up to Adrian's standards meant few, if any, matches. So, in order to remain active in the wrestling world, it has been necessary for Adrian to face such "uncouth rivals" as Dusty Rhodes, Black Jack Mulligan, and Dick Murdock, about whom Streets says, with an obvious air of superiority, "Look at the places these rednecks frequent. They have all these electric bulls, and people stand around drinking beer right out of the cans and bottles."

Street's words and actions may earn him the title of sissy, but who can argue with the success of the Exotic One, both in and out of the ring? Not only has he more than held his own with some of wrestling's biggest names, but he also has had several big parts in productions on the stage and screen, most notably in the blockbuster *Quest for Fire.* He also has written and recorded a single on his own Exotic label, called "I'm in Love with Me."

Adrian's 20-year career has elicited more than a little displeasure from his so-called uncouth opponents and the fans he calls "common." But no one can dispute that the unique blend of artistry and skill he has brought to the squared circle have enriched it, as it has him.

Below: Adrian Street takes up his position on the corner of Bobby Jaggers. Opposite: Adrian Street goes one way over Barry Windham's knee.

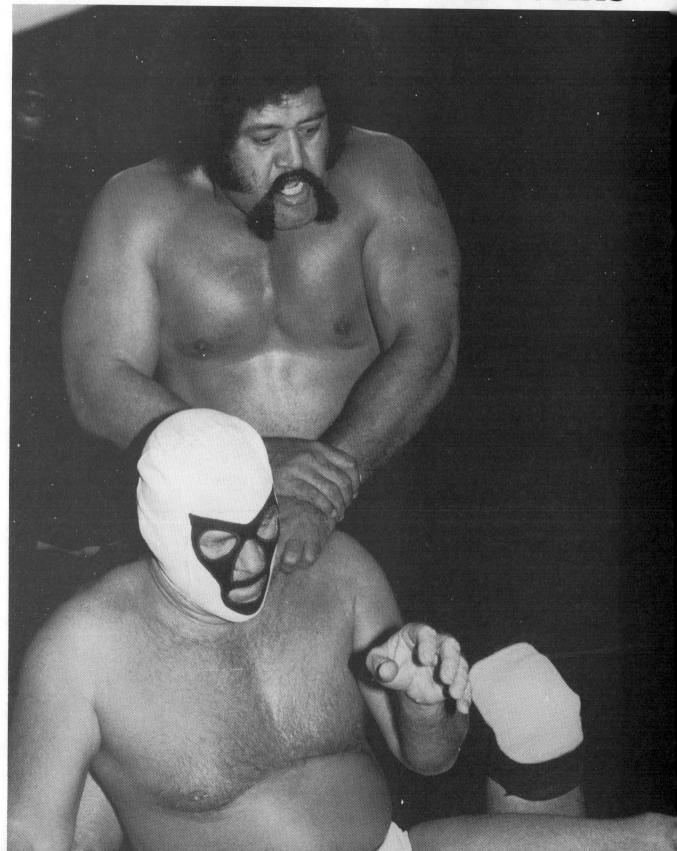

THE WILD
SAMOANS

THE ISLAND OF SAMOA IN THE sunny Pacific Ocean has brought us Afa and Sika, better known throughout wrestling circles as the Wild Samoans.

For the past ten years the Samoans have brought nothing but destruction and disorder to the wrestling scene. Their accomplishments in tag team wrestling have been surpassed by no other team in the sport. They've held the WWF tag team title on three occasions, as well as tag team titles in the Southeast and California.

For most of their careers the Samoans have been managed by "Captain" Lou Albano—who always manages to bring out the craziest in them. Late in 1983 Afa and Sika were joined by Samola, a younger member of their tribe. Although only 19 at the time, Samola had the size and strength to step right in and efficiently work with his island brothers. Yet he also added another dimension to the Samoan combination: youth. Now it's quite likely that the Samoans will continue to carry on their winning tradition for a long time to come.

Late in 1983, after holding the WWF tag team title for over a year, the Samoans lost their coveted title to Tony Atlas and Rocky Johnson. Manager Lou Albano was highly annoyed that the Samoans had lost "his" championship. The Captain continued to manage the team, but something was wrong. After Dick Murdoch and Adrian Adonis won the WWF tag title from Atlas and Johnson, things grew worse. Albano openly courted the new champions, hoping that they would join his stable.

This did not sit well with the Samoans. Unbeknownst to Albano, the Samoans requested a championship bout against

Opposite: One half of the Wild Samoans gives Wrestling II whole hell. Above: Sika shows Eddie Gilbert how wild the Samoans are.

Adonis and Murdoch. When the match was scheduled for June in Madison Square Garden, the Captain didn't know what to do. Needless to say, the fans sided with the Samoans.

Although they are now cheered, Afa, Sika, and Samola are still the same crazy and insane Samoans. And they always will be.

THE WOMEN

Fabulous Moolah is a pain in Jill Fontaine's neck.

FABULOUS MOOLAH

SHE'S FABULOUS MOOLAH, and she's the undisputed queen of women's wrestling. For 28 years she has dominated the women's wrestling scene, undefeated in title competition until 1984 and without peer.

The Fabulous One began her career as the humble servant of the Elephant Boy. In 1954 she made her wrestling debut in Massachusetts and was so well received in her premiere performance that she was invited to enter a championship tournament in Baltimore. Surprisingly, she advanced to the finals and then, wonder of wonders, defeated the reigning queen, June Byers. Until July 1984 she held the title she won that night, the longest dynasty in the history of sports.

With the determination to stay at the top, Moolah is unmatched in both energy and desire. Her burning ambition is to reclaim her reign as the best woman wrestler in the world, something to which she devotes all her time and attention. Some attribute her remarkable staying power to just this determination to be on top at any and all costs. Others cite her mind and body control, which she achieves through an Eastern technique she learned in the 1950's. And there are even some who believe her success is due to a secret potion concocted by Carolina backwoodsmen.

Moolah refutes all this as nonsense and says her success is based on three things: a desire for fame and wealth, toughness, and experience. But whatever the reasons for the Fabulous Moolah's staying power, one thing is certain: she has been able to do it before and continues to do it, time and again. For how much longer, no one knows. Only time and the Fabulous Moolah will determine that. But for the moment there's only one word to describe her, and that's *fabulous*!

Judy Martin knows the ropes—and is about to be shown them by Fabulous Moolah.

WOMEN'S WRESTLING

WHEN YOU TALK ABOUT women's wrestling, the Fabulous Moolah is the first person who comes to mind. But there are countless others who have made quite a name for themselves in professional wrestling.

"The Dallas Cowgirl," Wendi Richter, is the new reigning queen on the wrestling circuit. Richter reached immortality when she defeated the Fabulous Moolah in July 1984 in Madison Square Garden, ending Moolah's 28-year reign as champion. Moolah finally went down to defeat when Wendi Richter pinned her shoulders to the mat. Many claim that the victory would not have been possible without the help of rock 'n' roll sensation Cyndi Lauper, who was in Wendi's corner when the victory occurred. Nevertheless, Wendi Richter attained a goal that had eluded many, many others since 1957, the year the Fabulous Moolah originally captured the world women's title.

Other champions on the women's circuit include US champion Judy Martin and world tag team champions Princess Victoria and Velvet McIntyre. Judy Martin is an accomplished wrestler; she's rough and tough and knows exactly what to do to keep her title. She's cut from the same mold as the Fabulous Moolah. With her background and temperament she could be champion for a long time.

Princess Victoria and Velvet McIntyre are the darlings of the mat. Both have been wrestling for several years and began their careers in Canada. They are an excellent team with a thorough knowledge of the sport.

A newcomer to the women's scene is beautiful Desiree Petersen. Desiree started wrestling in Europe, but she is now a big star

Opposite: Velvet McIntyre lowers the boom on Judy Grable. Above: Wrestling queen Wendi Richter and rock queen Cyndi Lauper. Below: Peggy Lee makes Velvet McIntyre sing out—in pain.

in the United States. Desiree has the moves to make it all the way to the top.

In addition to the stars previously mentioned, there are many other top wrestlers on the circuit today. Included among this group are Peggy Lee, Carol Summers, Sherri Martel, Vivian St. John, Evelyn Stevens, Susan Green, and Hawaiian sensation Lelani Kai.

The women wrestlers never fail to excite the crowds with their wild, nonstop action. As Cyndi Lauper's song says, "Girls just want to have fun," and the ladies prove this fact in the ring every night of the week.

THE LEGENDS

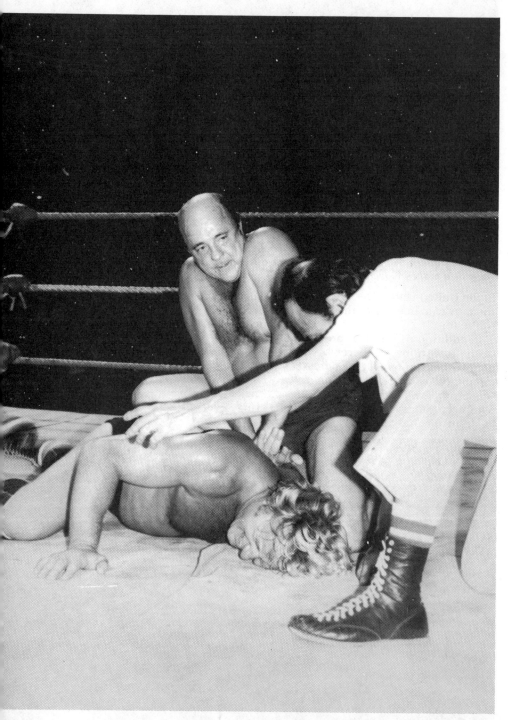

Above: Verne Gagne, one of the greatest of the greats, treats Nick Bockwinkel with disrespect. Opposite: The pride of a world champion.

MINNESOTA NATIVE VERNE Gagne is one of the all-time greats in the wrestling profession. Gagne was an excellent amateur wrestler before he turned to the professional ranks, and once he did his career took off. Gagne's first major accomplishment was winning the NWA junior title, which he defended for several years, and he followed this up by winning the prestigious AWA title, a title that he was to hold on and off for the next 20 years.

In his career Verne Gagne proved to be the greatest of the exponents of scientific wrestling techniques, and he has passed on this gift to many of today's top professionals. During the past 10 years Verne Gagne is credited with having taught the ropes to such stars as NWA champion Ric Flair, former WWF champion Bob Backlund, Jim Brunzell, Ken Patera, Rick Steamboat, Buddy Rose, and countless others.

Today this legend lives on in his son Greg, who is carrying on the great Gagne tradition. Greg is cut from the same mold as his illustrious father and has captured the AWA world tag team title three times, with his close friend Jim Brunzell. Greg, however, is hoping that someday he will be able to bring the AWA title back into the Gagne household.

Verne Gagne is a true credit to the wrestling profession. Over the years Verne has done much to champion the cause of professional wrestling, and his numerous awards, titles, and achievements will always be remembered by everyone throughout the wrestling world.

VERNE GAGNE

THERE IS ONLY ONE MAN truly worthy of the name "Killer," and that is Wladek "Killer" Kowalski. In his day there wasn't a wrestler in the sport who was more feared, more despised, or more respected.

If you question a veteran of the sport as to who his toughest opponent was, the name Killer Kowalski would probably be a most popular answer. "I've wrestled many tough men in my career," recalls the great Bruno Sammartino, "but no one was as vicious, as rough, or as tough as Killer." This opinion is shared by many.

What made him so fearless, so terribly awesome? It was his ability to go into the ring and give it all to come out on top—even if that meant biting, kick-

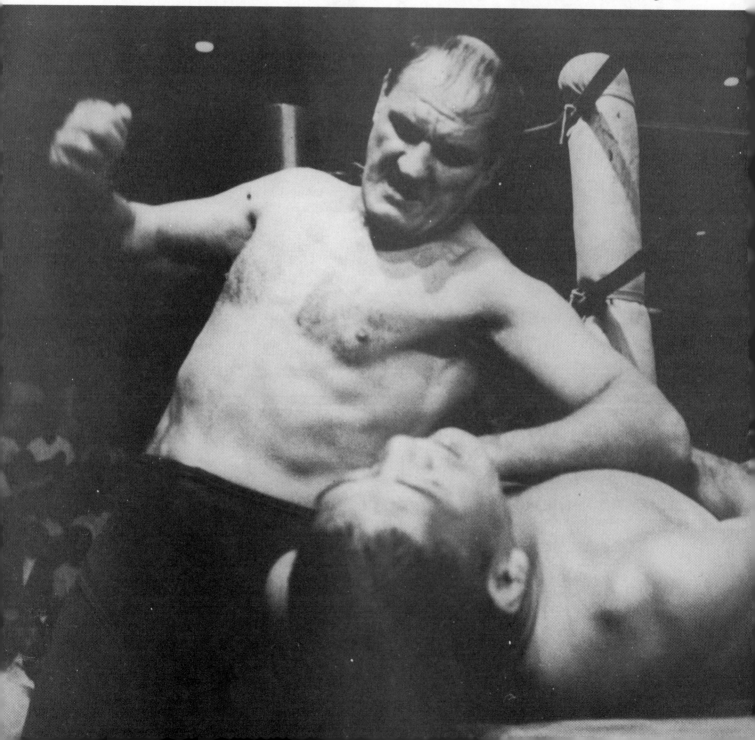

"KILLER" KOWALSKI

ing, clawing, and gouging. Anything went as far as he was concerned—as long as his arm was raised in victory at the end of the match. "I would use anything in my power to knock my opponent into submission. Only winners make the big bucks,

and I was determined always to be a winner."

The incident that established his reputation as a mauler occurred in 1954. In a match against Yukon Eric, Kowalski mounted the ring post, and with his feared flying knee drop, came crashing down onto the mat, severing Yukon Eric's ear in the process. After this bout, the legend of Killer Kowalski began to spread like brushfire. Kowalski claims that he didn't intentionally try to maim Yukon Eric, but he was also glad of the psychological advantage it gave him over his opponents from then on.

During his illustrious career Killer Kowalski traveled all over the world and won titles everywhere that he appeared. In fact, he was in such demand that he wrestled in more countries than any other wrestler of his era. He appeared in Australia, Indonesia, Malaysia, Singapore, Hong Kong, Japan, England, France, South Africa, and many other countries.

But aside from his wild ring tactics, Killer Kowalski is surprisingly mild-mannered and soft-spoken. Mention the name Killer Kowalski and visions of a wild man come to mind, a man capable of tearing his opponents limb from limb. And that is indeed a true picture of the Killer Kowalski in the ring, yet once he is away from the wrestling arena, Kowalski is ever articulate and gentle, the perfect gentleman. One might say of Killer Kowalski that he has a personality not unlike that of Dr. Jekyll and Mr. Hyde.

Killer still resides in the Boston area, where he now operates a school for aspiring young wrestlers. He also often serves as a special guest referee for the Eastern States Championship

Wrestling organization.

Killer Kowalski is one of the men who made this sport what it is today. He was a wrestler the fans loved to hate, an opponent to be feared, a competitor to be heralded as one of the first truly great superstars of wrestling.

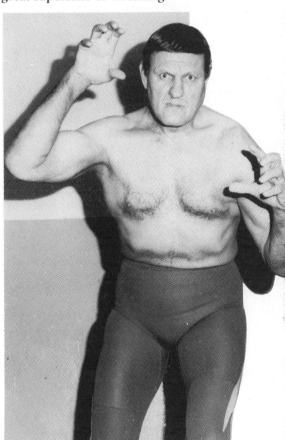

What becomes a legend, "Killer" Kowalski, most.

"Killer" Kowalski uses his special persuader on the Giant Baba.

ANTONINO ROCCA

ANTONINO ROCCA WAS BORN in Treviso, Italy, on April 23, 1923. He later moved to Argentina with his family, and it was there that "the master of the drop kick" first began learning his trade. He soon wrestled all over Europe, but won his first professional title at the age of 17 in Buenos Aires.

He journeyed to the United States in the late 1940's, arriving in New York, and immediately he began resurrecting wrestling to a profession of respectability. He was quite influential in changing the style of wrestling from simple hand-to-hand combat to that of high-flying, acrobatic, and elegant maneuvers. His charm and charisma, and, of course, his ability, pushed him quickly to the number-one spot in the hearts of the fans. "Next to Milton Berle, Rocca sold more TV sets than anyone else," stated one promoter. This statement sums up his incredible drawing power.

Rocca's accomplishments inside the ring are legendary. Those fortunate enough to have seen the great Rocca battle such men as the Graham brothers, "Killer" Kowalski, Buddy Rogers, Eduard Carpentier, and the Kangaroos will never forget this man in action.

He stayed on top of the wrestling world until the mid-1960's, and then his activities began to taper off. He accepted fewer and fewer matches, and was content to stay at home. In 1968 he announced his retirement and returned to his homeland to enjoy the memories of a long and successful career.

Rocca stayed out of sight until 1975, when he returned to do color commentary on a wrestling program on the East Coast. In this capacity a whole new generation of fans was in-

Rocca and Miguel Perez, two of wrestling's heroes of yesteryear.

troduced to the magnificent Antonino Rocca.

Although Rocca never completely came out of retirement, he did wrestle several more times, once in Los Angeles, once in Japan, and also in Puerto Rico. In Puerto Rico, on September 11, 1976, Rocca and his faithful partner, Miguel Perez, actually succeeded in capturing the North American tag team title from the Infernos. Twenty years had passed since these two had first won a title together, but the magic was obviously still there.

They lost their title to Gordon Nelson and Higo Hamaguchi, and Rocca returned home to concentrate on his du-

ties as color man for the WWF. On February 17, 1977, he was honored in Staten Island by promoter Tommy Dee on Antonino Rocca Night. He signed autographs for over an hour and then refereed the main event. A capacity crowd turned out to honor this living legend, and as it turned out, this was to be his last appearance. Two days later he was admitted to Roosevelt Hospital, and there he died, quietly.

Rocca's accomplishments in the wrestling world remain unsurpassed. All those who grew to know and love the man will never forget him. He was truly an all-time great, as a wrestler and as a person.

Antonino Rocca uses his famed drop kick to the chops of Gene Kiniski.

BUDDY ROGERS

The great Buddy Rodgers poses proudly in his championship belt.

SINCE WRESTLING CAME INTO prominence on television in the early 1950's, there have been thousands of stars flashed on the screen, thousands that may have been referred to as superstars in one sense or another. But the wrestling world has produced very few mega-stars. Buddy Rogers, known for his arrogant strut, his cocky mannerisms, and his long golden locks, is a true superstar, a mega-star to be remembered.

"Nature Boy" Buddy Rogers was one of the very top men in the young sport of wrestling. He is the only man ever to hold both the NWA and the WWF world titles. Throughout the late 1940's and the 1950's Buddy Rogers was a dominant force in the wrestling community. Rogers captured the prestigious NWA US heavyweight belt in 1959, and proudly defended it all around the country. In 1961 he rose to international fame with his defeat of Pat O'Conner in Chicago's Comiskey Park to win the NWA world heavyweight title.

Early in 1963 the WWF was inaugurated and the Federation held a tournament to determine its first titleholder. Buddy Rogers and the late, great Antonino Rocca were the two finalists. Rogers and Rocca battled it out in one of the classic duels of all time, and when the duel was done, Buddy Rogers emerged victorious, adding the WWF title to his already quite respectable résumé.

All champions must have their days, however, and Roger's downfall took place in 1963. The pressures of defending two titles began to take a toll on Buddy, and that year he lost his NWA crown to former champ Lou Thesz. Then, on May 17, 1963, in the old Garden, Buddy Rogers lost his re-

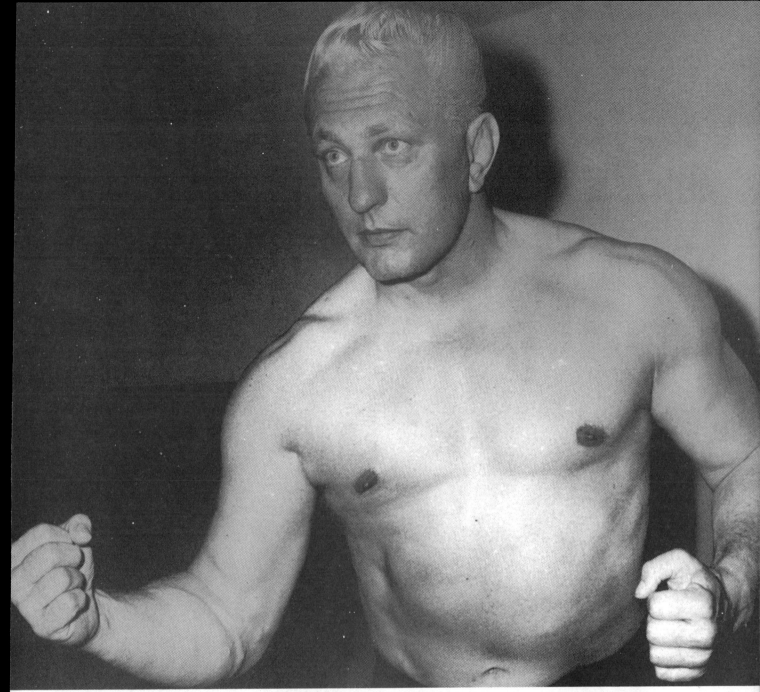

maining crown, the WWF title, to Bruno Sammartino in a mere 47 seconds. Rogers wrestled just once more in the Garden before he announced his retirement from the sport.

At one time or another Rogers wrestled all the greats of the past: Johnny Valentine, Bob Ellis, Antonino Rocca, Killer Kowalski, the Crusher, Yvon Roberts, Eduardo Carpentier, Bobby Mangoff, Bearcat Wright, Bobo Brazil, and many more. And during his illustrious career Buddy Rogers held many titles, including the Pacific Coast title, Texas heavyweight title, the East Coast title, the Ca-

nadian championship, and the US title, as well as every regional title in the country. Rogers also held the tag team championship on several occasions with his partners "Handsome" Johnny Barend and the "Big O" Bob Orton. Everywhere Rogers appeared he was a huge success.

Rogers's career was a flamboyant one, and he was one of the all-time great innovators in the sport. He was instrumental in introducing such moves as the pile driver, the atomic drop, and the world-famous figure-four leglock. The figure four was Rogers's "bread and but-

Buddy Rogers took on all the best.

ter" hold, and when he applied a figure-four lock, no one could break free. Several wrestlers claim that they could break out of the hold, but the fact remains that no one ever did.

Today, although he has retired from actual wrestling, Buddy Rogers has not left the wrestling scene completely. He has managed Jimmy "Superfly" Snuka and is looking for a new protégé. The fans are happy to have him back in the spotlight. Once a champion, always a champion. No one will ever forget the great Nature Boy.

BRUNO SAMMARTINO

THERE WILL NEVER BE AN-
other wrestler like Bruno Sammartino. When you hear of "the
Living Legend," only one man
comes to mind. Never has another wrestler dominated the
scene more than the magnificent Bruno Sammartino. Bruno
is in a class of his own.

He began wrestling in the late
1950's, and during the 1960's
and 1970's there was no one
who could top the great Italian.
His first claim to fame was on
May 17, 1963, when he de-
feated "Nature Boy" Buddy
Rogers for the WWF heavy-
weight title in an astounding 47
seconds. From then on until
January 1971 the Italian strongman was invincible and defeated every major wrestler in
the sport during his glorious
reign, including such greats as
"Killer" Kowalski, Johnny Valentine, Bill Watts, Fritz Von Erich,
Fred Blassie, John Tolas, and
Lou Thesz. But on January 18,
1971, Bruno lost his coveted title to Ivan Koloff, "the Russian
Bear," in an upset. Although
there was some question con-
cerning the pin, Bruno never
contested the decision.

Bruno stayed home for a
while after that match and spent
time with his family. But after
nearly a two-year layoff, he was
anxious to return to wrestling
and began making guest appear-
ances throughout the country.
This stage of semiretirement
lasted for one year, and then the
Italian was back in the old
groove again, wrestling more
and more often in the WWF
area. Bruno Sammartino made
history again on December 10,
1973, when he defeated Stan
Stasiak for the WWF title in
Madison Square Garden. During
the next few years Sammartino
defeated such foes as George
Steele, Ernie Ladd, "Mad Dog"
Vachon, Don Leo Jonathon,

Sammartino gives Ivan Koloff a little of his own medicine in a Russian chain match.

"Killer" Kowalski, Spiros Ari-
on, and Waldo Von Erich. But,
unfortunately, Bruno suffered a
serious neck injury in a match
against big Stan Hansen. It was
feared that the champion might
have suffered permanent injury,
but he came back for a rematch
and thoroughly thrashed Stan
Hansen in a wild brawl in Shea
Stadium.

Bruno's reign finally came to
an end on April 30, 1977, in the
Baltimore Civic Center. "Superstar" Billy Graham was the rob-
ber who stole his crown. The
match was riddled with controversy and confusion, but Bruno
never once complained about
the outcome. Bruno and Graham faced each other several
other times, but the Legend was
never able to reclaim his title.

Bruno once again went into
semiretirement, wrestling only
occasionally for the next few
years. He began a new career,
however, as color commentator
on the WWF televised wrestling
program.

Things went smoothly for the
great Sammartino for several
years, and then he became involved in a torrid feud with
former friend Larry Zbyszko.
The Zbyszko-Sammartino feud
went on for six months, ending
in August 1980, with a wild
cage match in Shea Stadium.
The fans went home happy after Bruno showed his stuff and
proved that he was indeed the
superior wrestler.

Bruno wrestled off and on
during the next year, but it was
obvious that his fighting spirit
was gone. The end of an era occurred on October 4, 1981,
when Bruno defeated George
"the Animal" Steele in a fare-
well match in the New Jersey
Meadowlands.

There will probably never be
another wrestler as talented,
loved, and respected as the
great Bruno Sammartino. But
we are happy he has been such
an important part of wrestling
for so long.

The great Bruno Sammartino.

LOU THESZ

SIX-TIME NWA WORLD HEAVY-weight champion Lou Thesz has been a part of the professional wrestling world for 50 years. For 18 of those years the legendary Thesz was champion of the world. Although Harley Race is one up on Thesz, having held the title seven times, Thesz has still held the title for a longer time period than Race.

On December 20, 1937, Thesz rose to national fame by defeating Everett Marshall in St. Louis to win the NWA title for the first time. Coached by Ed "Strangler" Louis, Ray Steel, and three-time Olympic winner George Tragos, the young Thesz's reign lasted only two months, but he quickly bounced back, and on February 23, 1939, he once against defeated Everett Marshall in St. Louis to regain the title. This time Thesz held the title four months.

It took another eight years before Lou Thesz returned to the top, but on April 25, 1947, he did, defeating "Whipper" Bill Watson. He held the honored position until November 21, 1947, when he was upended by Bill Longson. Then, on July 20, 1948, Thesz defeated Longson and held onto the title for the following eight years. At the time television was in its infancy, and Thesz soon became the most watched man on TV. His eight-year reign came to an end on March 15, 1957, when he was defeated by Bill Watson in Toronto. But Thesz was not washed up yet. He regained the title for a fifth time on November 9 of the same year. After he lost it the next time, it took another six years before he regained the NWA crown for the sixth and final time by ousting "Nature Boy" Buddy Rogers. Thesz held the title for 3 more years, making a total of 18 years that he was champion.

Lou Thesz has faced every top professional in the sport during his illustrious career. Some were exceptional wrestlers, others extraordinary performers. "Buddy Rogers was the best performer we ever had," Lou reminisces. "I think Jimmy Snuka is the best performer today." Among those that Thesz would rank in the "exceptional" category are Everett Marshall, Dick Hutton, and "Whipper" Watson.

Lou is still quite involved in wrestling. He often travels to San Antonio, St. Louis, and Mexico to referee bouts, and he also works with Southwest Championship Wrestling.

When he's not on the road, the six-time champion can be found relaxing with his wife, Charlie, in their Virginia Beach home. He loves sailing and fishing and has become a true outdoorsman.

Louis Thesz is a true credit to his sport.

The legendary Lou Thesz.

ACKNOWLEDGMENTS

This important work would not have been possible without the able assistance of the following people: Jacqueline Quartarano, Jack O'Shea, E. J. Geary, Bobby Meredith, J. B. Randolph Sugar, Hedy Caplan, Diane Cook, and Deborah Weiss. To them, and to you, we can only say, "Thanks."